KU-686-781

The Spread of Sponsorship

IN THE ARTS, SPORT, EDUCATION, THE HEALTH SERVICE & BROADCASTING

EDITED BY

SIR ROY SHAW

1240092 ·

LIBRARY

ACC. No.	DEPT.
00994389	d

CLASS No.

658 .1522 SHA

UNIVERSITY
COLLEGE CHESTER

BLOODAXE BOOKS

Introduction copyright © Roy Shaw 1993
Copyright of essays rests with authors as listed opposite © 1993

ISBN: 1 85224 190 X

First published 1993 by
Bloodaxe Books Ltd,
P.O. Box 1SN,
Newcastle upon Tyne NE99 1SN.

Bloodaxe Books Ltd acknowledges
the financial assistance of Northern Arts.

LEGAL NOTICE

All rights reserved. No part of this book may be
reproduced, stored in a retrieval system, or
transmitted in any form, or by any means, electronic,
mechanical, photocopying, recording or otherwise,
without prior written permission from Bloodaxe Books Ltd.

Requests to publish work from this book
must be sent to Bloodaxe Books Ltd.

Roy Shaw has asserted his right under
Section 77 of the Copyright, Designs and Patents Act 1988
to be identified as the editor of this work.

Cover printing by J. Thomson Colour Printers Ltd, Glasgow.

Printed in Great Britain by
Cromwell Press Ltd, Broughton Gifford, Melksham, Wiltshire.

CONTENTS

CONTRIBUTORS

Roy Shaw advised Britain's first arts minister, Labour's Jennie Lee, and her Tory successor Lord Eccles, when he was Professor of Adult Education at Keele University. He was appointed a member of the Arts Council in 1973 and became Secretary-General in 1975. He was knighted in 1979, retired in 1983, and has since published *The Arts and the people* (1987) and many articles on arts policy.

Tony Cook is a 40 year old journalist with a wide ranging track record. He has worked in television, radio and newspapers, most notably as an associate producer on the *Dispatches* programme *Sick at Heart*, about lack of exercise by children; as a researcher on the award-winning *Secret History*; as Editor of IRN International and Network Editor for IRN and *News on Sunday*. He also presented *Talking Sport*, his own nightly sports show on London Talkback Radio. He is now a director of Praxis Films.

Francis Beckett writes on education for the *Guardian*, the *Observer*, the *Wall Street Journal Europe* and the *Times Educational Supplement*. His book about the British Communist Party is to be published in 1994.

Michael O'Connor is a consultant in public health policy working on a wide range of initiatives including consultancy for the World Health Organisation in Eastern Europe. Previously he was a civil servant, when his duties included being Private Secretary to two Ministers of Health. He has also been the Director of a pressure group, the Coronary Prevention Group.

Michael Rayner is the Co-ordinator for the British Heart Foundation Coronary Prevention Project based within the Department of Public Health and Primary Care at the University of Oxford. The aim of this project is to research into health policy in relation to the prevention of coronary heart disease, focusing on food advertising, food labelling and health education. From 1986 to 1993 he was Senior Research Officer for the Coronary Prevention Group and prior to that a Wellcome Research Fellow at the Welcome Unit for the History of Medicine at Oxford University. He has published numerous reports and articles on health topics ranging from in vitro fertilisation to the Common Agricultural Policy.

Tim Leggatt was Director of Broadcasting Research Unit in 1988-91. He is now a communication consultant and has worked for the BBC and for NHK, the Japanese broadcasters. His most recent writing in the field has concerned the assessment of quality in television. He is based in Brussels.

ROY SHAW

Introduction

In the 1980s business sponsorship spread into many areas of our national life and in the nineties seems set to grow still further. The market research analysts Mintel estimate that in 1991 the total sponsorship spend was £325 million, with at least as much again spent on 'promotional support'. This book offers the first critical overview of the five main areas of sponsorship.

The term 'sponsorship' is often misused or misunderstood, so it may be helpful to begin by defining it. The Oxford Dictionary still tells us that a sponsor is primarily someone who answers for an infant at baptism, but adds that in 1931 the name was given to a business firm which paid for a broadcast which introduced advertisements for its product.

Today, the title of sponsor is often given to anyone who gives money or help in any of the five fields covered by this book. By that definition the editor is himself a sponsor and so is the Arts Council. However, in the world of business sponsorship it is generally agreed that we should make a distinction between, on the one hand funding bodies like the Arts Council and donors or patrons who make philanthropic gifts, and on the other hand sponsors who see their expenditure as a business cost from which they expect a good return in the form of publicity or advertising.

Sponsorship was well defined in a government leaflet devised in 1986 to encourage firms to sponsor the arts. Sponsorship, it was said, was 'a payment by a business firm...for the purpose of promoting its name, products or services. It is a commercial deal, not a philanthropic gift'. This came from the government's Office of Arts and Libraries, but the definition applies to all forms of sponsorship and has not been bettered.

In other words, sponsorship is a form of advertising. The Inland Revenue regards it as advertising, allowing expenditure on it to be set off against a company's tax liability as money spent 'wholly and exclusively for the purpose of trade'. Any hint of philanthropic purpose would make the expenditure ineligible for tax relief.

In spite of that, the fact that sponsorship *is* advertising is not generally understood. For example, the British Social Attitudes Survey found that in 1991 nearly two-thirds of the population wanted cigarette advertising to be banned, but less than half would support a ban on cigarette firms' sponsorship of arts and sports. We hope this book will help remove that confusion.

Sports and arts are the most conspicuous areas of sponsorship and the following chapters show that in both areas sponsors believe they are buying a cheap and very effective form of advertising. In these fields and in education and health, practitioners are forced to rely increasingly on sponsorship because government funding is inadequate and compares very unfavourably with that provided by the governments of our main European neighbours.

Although well established in other fields, sponsorship was illegal on television until 1991. It has already grown considerably since then and, controversially, the book ends with a forecast that viewers may benefit from this growth, despite fears to the contrary. However, the general question raised by the book is whether it is desirable that crucial areas of our national life should increasingly become adjuncts of commercial advertising.

ROY SHAW

Sponsoring the Arts

Until the Second World War, the arts, particularly the performing arts, had to survive on what they could earn at the box office. During that war, the government came to realise that the arts made an important contribution to public morale and that they needed extra funding. In the past they had been patronised by kings, the church and the aristocracy, but in a democratic age support should come from the taxpayer. At the end of the war, all parties in parliament agreed to continue the wartime arts funding and set up the Arts Council of Great Britain. This was an independent body acting as an intermediary between government and the arts, thus ensuring that the arts were free from political interference.

This system continues to the present day and under it the arts in Britain have achieved worldwide renown. For over a quarter of a century it was almost the sole source of arts funding, apart, of course, from the box office. Sponsorship was virtually unknown; it originated in America, but even there barely existed thirty years ago. Most businessmen still believed that 'the business of business is business', but by 1965, ideas were changing and the New York Board of Trade held a discussion of the question 'Is culture the business of business?' They came to the conclusion that it was and sponsorship began.

Eleven years later, it had hardly begun in the UK, but Jennie Lee, our first Minister for the Arts, wrote that the industrial patron was the heir to the now virtually extinct wealthy private patron of the past. Stressing that we now faced a task which rarely concerned the private patron, that of ensuring that the arts were made more widely available, she looked to industry and commerce to play their part. So far, she noted, industry had done little, but she hoped that patronage of the arts would come to be regarded as a form of enlightened self interest. We would now speak of sponsorship rather than patronage, but in 1966 the distinction had not been drawn and even ten years later, as Colin Tweedy, the present Director General of the Association for Business Sponsorship of the Arts (ABSA) has observed, 'there was a surprising degree of business naiveté. Few firms could distinguish between a donation and a sponsorship deal.' As we shall see, almost every firm can now, but the public perception is far less clear.

ABSA was not founded until 1976 and to its credit it began by making a clear distinction between old-fashioned patronage or philanthropy on the one hand and sponsorship on the other, where business expected a good return in the form of publicity. ABSA's task was to encourage sponsorship of the arts and to promote public acceptance of the idea of sponsorship. The then Labour Minister for the Arts (Hugh Jenkins) gave his blessing to the enterprise.

The founding chairman of ABSA was Tony Garrett, then Chairman of Imperial Tobacco, and the organisation's first office was located in his firm's headquarters. He later confessed that he thought 'it would do no harm' to the image of Imperial Tobacco to be associated with such a body. An advisory council was formed and Lord Goodman who had been (among many other things), a distinguished chairman of the Arts Council, became its chairman. To some, it seemed that Lord Goodman had 'changed sides', but he was and remains a believer in plural funding, based on a partnership of government subsidy and business support.

'An idea whose time has come'

When I retired from the post of Arts Council Secretary General in 1983, there was much surprise when Luke Rittner, the Director of ABSA, succeeded me. The marriage between public subsidy and business sponsorship seemed to have been well and truly consummated, but it was to prove one in which sponsorship flourished rather more than subsidy, for it was enthusiastically promoted by all of Mrs Thatcher's arts ministers. The first, Norman St John Stevas (now Lord Fawsley), hailed sponsorship as 'an idea whose time has come' and he warned the arts world that it had to come to terms with the fact that government policy 'had decisively tilted away from the expansion of the public sector to the enlargement of the private sector'. (By the private sector he meant not individual giving, but business sponsorship.)

He threw himself enthusiastically into boosting the sponsorship idea, even doing ABSA's job for it by urging businessmen to sponsor, reminding them that sponsorship 'has its roots in marketing, public relations and advertising'. Subsequent ministers followed his example and in 1984, Richard Luce introduced the Business Sponsorship Incentive Scheme, through which government matched first time and existing sponsors when they put up new money for the arts. The government pays ABSA to administer the scheme and Colin Tweedy wrote in 1987 that these additional funds had transformed ABSA, making it possible to appoint additional staff outside London. In that same year many observers were discerning what I said (in *The Arts and the people*, 1987) might be 'the twilight of the Arts Council'.

However, the amount of public subsidy for the arts, taking the Arts Council's disbursements and those of Local Government, is still over £400 million. The latest estimated sum spent by sponsors is £57 million. So public subsidy is still more than seven times larger than the amount contributed by sponsors. It is difficult to discover the precise amounts given by individual sponsors. Indeed they are often coy about revealing them, perhaps because they frequently gain very impressive publicity for comparatively modest amounts. The *Financial Times*, a newspaper favourable to sponsorship and the only one with a sponsorship correspondent, headed one of its regular articles on sponsorship *The art of getting cheap publicity*.

The Arts Council has the detailed budgets of all the arts organisations which it funds and in its 1991/2 annual report it provides details of the three main sources of income. They compare as follows:

	DANCE	DRAMA	LITERATURE	MUSIC	VISUAL ARTS
Arts Council Subsidy	48.5%	34.1%	26.2%	31.3%	30.7%
Sponsorship	10.2%	4.8%	1.5%	11.6%	18.2%
Box office and other earned income	35.9%	48.7%	69.2%	31.3%	37.9%

These figures demonstrate that the common impression that the arts now thrive mainly on sponsorship is far from the truth.

The image of sponsorship

Why do many people think that arts organisations depend mainly on sponsorship when the figures show clearly that this is not the case? It is because sponsors, through their advertising departments, are very determined to get 'top billing'. Sometimes an event's publicity will say that it has 'been made possible' by a certain sponsor. To the casual observer, this can give the impression that the sponsor was *wholly* responsible for making the event possible. It is an impression which sponsors do nothing to discourage. A famous example is that of the Royal Opera House 'proms'. Once a year the stalls seats are removed and young people are able to buy a 'seat' (on the floor) for very much less than the normal cost. This is a very good idea and it is sponsored by the Midland Bank, who deserve due credit (i.e. publicity) for it. However, when I was Secretary General of the Arts Council, I was concerned to note that the bank was getting *undue* credit in the form of a large banner across the front of the Opera House proclaiming that the Proms were sponsored by the Midland Bank. More than one journalist commented that this gave the false impression that the Opera House, or at least the Proms, were wholly funded by the bank. I checked the figures and found that the bank was contributing about one seven hundredth of the annual amount paid to the Opera by the Arts Council. The bank's contribution was just 'top up' money.

I was invited to a tobacco company's launch of another opera sponsorship. The elaborate publicity again gave the impression of exclusive funding by the sponsor. This time, the Arts Council was giving thirty-two times as much 'to make possible' the opera events. On another occasion, Imperial Tobacco demanded of an opera touring company funded by the Arts Council that a visit to Bristol should be announced as 'their' tour. I spoke to the opera company about it and they were embarrassed. Yes, it was wrong, they admitted, but the sponsor had insisted on exclusive billing. I talked to the tobacco company, and they climbed down.

Even Royal Insurance, Britain's largest sponsor, giving £2.1 million to the Royal Shakespeare Company over three years, insists that on all the theatre company's literature (about four million pieces a year) its own name should appear boldly under the theatre company's name – in type almost as bold as 'Shakespeare'. You have to look rather carefully to discover at the bottom corner of some (not all) bills and leaflets, a diminutive logo saying 'Arts Council funded', yet the Arts Council's annual funding is £8.5 million a year compared with the insurance company's more £700,000.

While writing this, I came across two smaller but typical examples of a sponsor's greed for publicity. To many people's surprise, the Arts Council itself appointed a 'Sponsorship Manager'. Two sponsorships for events which this officer arranged in autumn 1991, for two different makes of beer, both give the impression that the events, though basically funded by the Council, are totally funded by the sponsor. One is a photographic competition in which the sponsor's name alone features in the logo. The other is a series of contemporary music concerts sponsored by Rolling Rock beer. The publicity proclaims these 'Rolling Rock Tours', and again you have to look very carefully to discover the Arts Council's and local authorities' funding role. When I suggested to the Council's sponsorship manager that this was rather odd, she looked puzzled, saying: 'That's the way it is'. It was obviously beyond her brief to consider 'Is that the way it ought to be?' One of the sponsors, in a press release, expresses satisfaction that the sponsorship not only promotes their beer, 'but also provides a wide range of promotional opportunities that can be tailored to suit all trade sectors'.

Sponsors often spend as much or more on advertising their sponsorship than they do on the sponsorship itself. In the old days of 'patronage' donors sometimes did good by stealth; now sponsors want every ounce of publicity they can get for their money, becoming indignant for example, when the media do not include their names in reviews of arts events. ABSA, on their behalf, puts pressure on the media to give the sponsors' credits. I have been asked by a theatre's sponsorship department to be sure to credit sponsors when I write a theatre column for a weekly journal. I don't, and nor do other critics, because most sponsored events are more heavily funded by the Arts Council and it would be invidious to name one and not the other and to name both on every occasion would make for monotonous reading. Moreover, Mintel's research showed that fewer than two out of ten consumers thought the sponsor should be named in press coverage.

It is very difficult for an arts organisation to complain about the sponsors' pressure for maximum publicity, even when these demands seem to go beyond the bounds of good taste. Several orchestras already perform on platforms adorned with banners or placards showing the sponsor's name. When he was Arts Minister, Lord Gowrie complacently rejoiced in the good taste of sponsors, saying 'You don't get *Traviata* sung in Texaco T-shirts'; but he did not hear, as I did, an exasperated sponsor asking a world conference on sponsorship, 'What's so sacrosanct about art?' (In 1980, I heard the Chairman of the BBC saying they would not show football with shirt-advertising. Three years later, they had accepted it.) About the same time, Luke Rittner (then at ABSA) was praising an orchestral sponsorship where 'the programmes are very smart – and look like packets of [the sponsor's] cigarettes...And it's very effective'. He did not mention that the orchestra players were wearing bow ties which were also in the sponsor's colours. In a 1991 production of Mozart's *Don Giovanni*, sponsored by an ice cream company, the first half ended with the cast smeared with the sponsor's ice cream. What indeed, is so sacrosanct about art?

It is, of course, easier for the large 'flagship' arts organisations to resist pressure from a sponsor, if only because their prestige means it will be easier for them to find an alternative sponsor. So Lord Rayne, when he was chairman of the National Theatre, not only rejected a sponsorship because of blatantly 'exclusive' advertising demands that accompanied it, but wrote to *The Times* to say that he was 'not prepared to see the National Theatre imply that it owes its existence to commercial enterprise for a hypothetical £750,000...while it is receiving eight times that amount from the nation'. In December 1992, however, the RSC apparently had no qualms about having advertising displays for margarine and washing powder in their Stratford foyer.

In the 70s, the Royal Opera felt able to reject a sponsorship deal under which girls would distribute samples of a product (I think it was perfume) in the auditorium, but the famous London Symphony Orchestra did accept sponsorship from a cigarette firm, allowing girls to give free cigarettes to people entering the concert hall. In addition, there was a large promotional banner behind the orchestra, whose members wore the cigarette sponsor's colours. For all that, the sponsor paid only 4% of the orchestra's costs. Asked what the firm expected to get in return, the orchestra's manager unhesitatingly replied: 'They expect to sell more cigarettes.' As a bonus, he might have added, they were getting an advertisement without the inconvenience of a government health warning.

It is therefore difficult to take seriously the sponsorship director of the Peter Stuyvesant Foundation (the cigarette firm concerned), when he claimed (*Arts Express*, 1986) that they don't measure commercial return, but are more concerned to support the arts. Sponsors often claim to be concerned to help the arts or to 'give something back to the community', but their money may have come from their advertising budget and can be set off against taxation precisely because (in the words of the Inland Revenue) it is money spent 'wholly and exclusively for the purpose of trade'.

Tobacco sponsorship

Peter Taylor's excellent book *The Smoke Ring* (1984) examines in damaging detail the tobacco industry's use of sponsorship of arts and sports. Sponsors sometimes make a distinction between sponsorships aimed at selling products and those aimed at burnishing a firm's image. However, the two functions obviously overlap: if the consumer feels good about a company (s)he is more likely to buy its products or services. The tobacco industry has a special image problem: the medical profession throughout the world has unanimously identified cigarette smoking as the most preventable cause of illness and premature death. Nearly twenty years ago, the government's Chief Medical Officer said of the tobacco industry, 'They know they're selling death.' In late 1991, the Health Education Authority reported that 110,000 people a year die from smoking related diseases – twelve every hour. Astonishingly, the tobacco industry professes to be unconvinced by the weight of medical evidence; but they do recognise that it gives them an image problem.

Sir Anthony Kershaw, MP, a tobacco executive who was also the company's paid parliamentary consultant (blessed word!) confessed to Peter Taylor that it was bad if tobacco firms seemed to be composed of 'hard-faced people who don't give a hang how many people die every year'. Hence the importance of sponsorship: as he put it 'Sponsorship makes us all good guys'. We may wonder whether it is right that the tobacco industry should through sponsorship be able to put on the appearance of being good guys? ABSA sees no problem here and neither does Lord Goodman, who once said: 'I will take money for the arts, sir, be it from murderers, rapists or anybody.' Lord Goodman is one of the wisest and most decent men I have ever known; he also likes making striking Johnsonian pronouncements and I'm afraid this is a nonsensical one which, if taken seriously, could be dangerous. It abdicates any moral responsibility when accepting sponsorship, and hard-up arts organisations are under heavy pressure to act on the principle that 'money is money – wherever it comes from'.

'Even if it comes from drug dealers or the IRA?' I asked a friend who was running a very successful regional theatre. Yes, he told me; if he were in Eire he probably would accept money from the IRA. The RSC's sponsorship officer summed up the predicament of the arts world. When challenged about the morality of a particular sponsorship, she answered: 'We cannot afford to have ethics like that.' Unsurprisingly, but sadly, in 1991, two thirds of the country's arts organisations said 'Yes' when asked whether they would accept money from tobacco companies.

The public affairs director of the Tobacco Advisory Council (funded by the industry) told *Arts Express* (June 1986) that although most tobacco money was focussed on sport, there was a trend to move towards the arts. Sport sponsorship was very good for reaching the broad mass of the people, he said, but 'arts sponsorship appeals to a more carefully defined group...a more discerning group – the opinion formers'. He went on to say that tobacco sponsorship was 'designed to present the company as a responsible company that is making something that has a quality about it'. That 'quality' includes the power to kill and cause many forms of illness, so it is not surprising that this spokesman added: 'It is not so incongruous to sponsor the arts.' It is not always less incongruous. Dame Kiri Ti Kanawa once said that she found it difficult to sing after being at a party where people smoked.

Philanthropy or advertising?

In its 1991 tax guide for sponsors, ABSA warns that to be allowed as a business expense and deducted from tax payable, sponsorship must yield a 'genuine commercial return (e.g. advertising)'. Nevertheless, arts bodies regularly and publicly express profuse thanks to their sponsors. No wonder in America sponsorship has been called 'phoney philanthropy'.

Ian Rushton, of Royal Insurance, told a journalist that he had not gone into sponsorship for philanthropic reasons, saying 'I *am*, after all, first and foremost a business man'. Royal Insurance's headquarters are in Liverpool, but apparently they do not feel obliged to spend much on sponsorship there: national exposure through the RSC makes better business sense. Even there, the company conducts 'exit polls' of theatre patrons to check whether their sponsorship is hitting the right targets – that is, people who are most likely to buy insurance from them.

All human motives tend to be a mixture of self-interest and altruism, and sponsors are human. There are, however, many statements on the record that show what the sponsor's prime motive is. The chief executive of Digital Equipment said (*The Times*, 4 May 1991) that 'We believe very clearly that the amount of money we've spent on the arts has more than repaid itself. We can measure the business we've got as a result of it. This is not the Salvation Army, this is business...' In the US, sponsors are equally forthright. In the mid-eighties, the retiring chairman of Philip Morris, the giant tobacco firm, confessed: 'Our fundamental interest in the arts is self interest...The decision to support the arts is not determined by the need or state of the arts. We are out to beat the competition.' The essence of the matter was put very frankly at a conference of sponsors at which, sitting as an observer, I heard one sponsor call on his colleagues to admit that their motives were 'enlightened self-interest'. This brought a fierce correction from another powerful sponsor: '*Brutal* self interest, you mean.'

Does sponsorship work – is it an efficient advertising medium? We have seen that some large sponsors are convinced that it is, though being a sponsor is such an enjoyable experience, that perhaps sponsors are not inclined to be too precise in measuring results. There is a problem in all forms of advertising, expressed in the old maxim attributed to more than one famous business head, that half of every advertising expenditure is wasted, but the trouble is, no one knows which half. As I write, the newspaper industry is conducting a campaign to persuade advertisers that a large part of the money spent on buying television commercials is wasted. There is little hard evidence of the effectiveness of arts sponsorship, though a commercial research organisation's examination of a Mars sponsorship of the London Marathon claimed that 'the shape of the claimed purchase/use line followed the sponsorship line almost exactly'.

The effect of sponsorship on the arts

It is easier to discern the effect of sponsorship on the arts than on a company's profits. Sponsorship is often accompanied by 'corporate entertainment' which will include drink (usually champagne), before, during and after a show. After a show, the sponsor's guests are often invited to a party 'to meet the stars'. Dinner before the show is not unusual and I have sat behind a row of black-tied men whose lady companions each had an identical box of chocolates on her lap. I have also sat near restless or conspicuously bored beneficiaries of corporate entertainment, but the journalist Sean French recorded amusingly (*New Statesman*, 24 March 1989) a worse experience. He went to the National Theatre to see *Hamlet* and found a private refreshment tent in the foyer, 'prudently surrounded by security men to prevent us groundlings from getting at the champagne'. Later, he sat next to a somnolent executive and was distracted by other 'guests' more interested in chatting among themselves than in watching the play and 'scrummaging among their crinkly sweet-wrappers'.

A few months after French's report of the unacceptable face of sponsorship, ABSA, having received other complaints, drafted guidelines for companies on how their staff and guests should behave at the theatre. These included not hogging the bar and not wearing evening dress if everyone else is in casual clothes, lest they risk becoming 'objects of ridicule'. Jennie Lee could scarcely have foreseen such a situation when, a quarter of a century earlier, she expressed the hope that business would help to make the arts more widely accessible. In general, it has had precisely the opposite effect, fostering a new form of black-tie elitism. To be fair, there are some exceptions to this generalisation, though they do not form a major part of sponsorship. BP has a long standing record of sponsoring arts for young people and educational ventures, while W.H. Smith in 1991 sponsored a summer school in literature for young people.

The time factor

Much as they need sponsors' money, many arts organisations find that getting it makes excessive demands on their time and effort. An American report (1991) found that 'everyone's favourite complaint is the time problem'. The larger organisations can afford to have special staff, formerly called sponsorship officers but now more often called development officers. The Royal National Theatre has a vigorous development department (see below), but nevertheless David Aukin, when he was the theatre's chief executive, told me that he and the artistic director had to spend two evenings a week entertaining actual or potential sponsors. After one such evening, Jaguar cars told him they would sponsor again 'If we can sell a couple of cars as a result'.

Peter Jonas, when he was Artistic Director of English National Opera, complained a few years ago that he had to spend about 15% of his time on fund-raising, while Terry Hands, the retiring Artistic Director of the RSC said that for five years he had spent 75% of his time on 'making money, raising money and saving money'. The burden of fund-raising (including sponsorship seeking) falls most heavily on smaller arts organisations. Anthony Beck of Liverpool University, who has made a special study of arts funding, reported in November 1991 that in smaller arts organisations on Merseyside 'sponsorship is just one job among many for the directors. All reported that increasing sponsorship significantly would take more time, effort and human resources than their institutions could provide. The financial return on the investment of time and energy made it an inefficient mode of fund raising.' An ABSA survey (1982) found that three-quarters of arts organisations did not have a designated fund-raiser.

Let Julian Spalding, Director of Glasgow Museums and Art Galleries, have the last word on this problem. He wrote (in 1989) that he and his like were 'scampering about, raising money from companies with large promotion budgets...and we have no time left to develop the heart of what we do'.

Another serious time factor problem in sponsorships is that they are often of short duration. The present Secretary General of the

Arts Council put the problem in a nutshell when he said 'Sponsorship comes and goes'. And its coming and going is determined not by the needs of the arts organisation, but by the needs (or wishes) of the sponsor. I heard a major sponsor tell a conference of colleagues: 'You should be absolutely ruthless in breaking off any sponsorship that does not fit your present needs'. By contrast, public subsidy is usually long term and on the rare occasions when it is withdrawn the reason has nothing to do with the self interest of the subsidising body. It may result from an adverse judgement on the arts organisation's artistic and/or administrative efficiency. It may also be caused by the inadequacy of the government's grant to the Arts Council. In either case it is an unusual event.

In 1991, the Arts Council was being severely criticised for giving too small a grant to the National Youth Theatre; at the same time, a decision by Sainsbury's to withdraw completely their sponsorship of the same theatre passed without notice. Apparently it is generally accepted that a sponsor has no more moral responsibility to continue a particular sponsorship than he would have to continue to advertise in a particular newspaper or other medium after that advertising had served its purpose. The *Financial Times'* sponsorship correspondent wrote (5 December 1988) of the 'debilitating danger of companies coming in on a 'one off' basis raising the expectation of an arts group only to let it down flat'. Twelve years earlier, Lord Redcliffe-Maud had warned (in his Gulbenkian report on *Support for the Arts*): 'The firms have no responsibility towards arts organisations and the latter could find themselves overnight in grave embarrassment if they became dependent to any great extent on business patronage.'

It is unusual for sponsorships to last more than two or three years and Luke Rittner, when he was Director of ABSA, said seven years was 'clearly much too long a time'. Gallachers have funded the Ulster Orchestra for over a decade and W.H. Smith have funded the Poetry Society's Poets in Schools scheme for 21 years, but these are quite exceptional. In 1991, ABSA instituted a special award for long-term sponsorships. The award went to a firm with a five-year record.

The fact that 'brutal self interest' underlies most (but not all) sponsorship deals gives an ironic ring to the declarations of profound gratitude to the sponsors to be found in many theatre and concert programmes and heard at many arts events. I have yet to hear sponsors decline such thanks on the grounds that they were only acting out of self interest and were looking for cheap and effective advertising. Conversely, I have never heard an arts organisation make a public criticism of a sponsor. The reason is obvious: the arts world cannot afford to alienate sponsors. To be fair, it is not too easy for arts organisations to criticise the Arts Council either, but it is far from impossible and wry jokes about 'biting the hand that feeds you' are common in the world of publicly subsidised arts.

In view of the foregoing, it is not surprising that years ago Luke Rittner admitted that sponsorship was 'fickle' or that Terry Hands of the RSC, looking at it from the other side, said sponsorship was 'inevitably capricious'. (His successor, Adrian Noble, describes it as 'volatile'.) Lord Rayne, who had been involved in the National Theatre's sponsorship deals, wrote when he retired that 'it is a hazardous business relying on sponsorship'.

Sponsorship and quality

Whereas public subsidy by the Arts Council takes account in making grant decisions of the quality of the work done by arts organisations or individuals, sponsors often have no means of assessing quality. Luke Rittner once admitted that 'many sponsored events have not been of the highest quality, they just happened to suit the sponsor'. He also put the same point in another way, saying that for the sponsor 'better' did not mean 'artistically better'.

Often, however, sponsors simply latch on to well established prestigious arts organisations such as the RSC, which specifically invites firms to sponsor them and thereby become 'synonymous with excellence'. It is a phrase to be pondered. Obviously, firms do not become excellent through sponsoring the RSC or the Royal Opera, but they can buy the *appearance* of excellence by doing it. Of course, advertisers have long sought to associate their services or products with artistic excellence. Years ago, Lux toilet soap used to advertise that five out of six glamorous film stars used their soap, inviting women to associate themselves with the glamour of the stars. Today, firms regularly use film or television stars to commend their products, often merely for voice-overs. A well-known actor told me he could earn more in a couple of days making a television commercial than he could from months of work in the theatre. The arts provide sponsors with a happy alternative to guilt by association: excellence by association.

The lengths to which even leading arts organisations will go to attract sponsors is remarkable. In 1989, the Royal National Theatre issued a very glossy brochure with a gilt-embossed title: 'The Royal

National Theatre SHARE OFFER'. The text promises that 'a share in this theatre is a high performance investment for any company. The returns are significant in terms of increased corporate awareness, enhanced public image, high profile media coverage and prestigious entertainment facilities.' Like the RSC, the RNT promises that its reputation for excellence 'reflects favourably on sponsoring companies'. Moreover, it offers 'access to opinion formers', explaining that nearly half the theatre's patrons are members of higher than average social groups. Finally, the 'prestige entertainment facilities' can provide anything from a simple reception to 'a full scale Gala' making the theatre 'the perfect venue for glamorous and memorable business entertainment'. A leading businessman is quoted as saying that· his firm's 'corporate contributors' evening' proved of unequalled value to his business.

Sponsorship and censorship

In 1986, the Arts Council commissioned an enquiry into professional theatre in England, which produced a report called *Theatre is for all*. The enquiry found that 'theatre companies are concerned that sponsorship may bring implicit censorship as the sponsor seeks the production which will most benefit his company's products or activities'.

Also testifying to the effect which the need to please a sponsor may have on arts organisations' work, Peter Hall has said that theatre directors now have to ask themselves not 'do we like this play', or even 'will the public like it', but 'will the sponsors like it'? The result is what I would prefer to describe as self-censorship. I know of a festival director who has been instructed to put on only events which will attract sponsorship. In 1988, I heard an American sponsorship consultant tell, as though it were a very funny story, of a small theatre company which approached a sponsor. 'What kind of plays do you do?' asked the potential sponsor and the theatre spokesman replied 'What kind of plays would you like us to do?' About the same time, the *Financial Times*' sponsorship correspondent was writing that 'companies are keen to sponsor the arts but increasingly they want their own tailor-made event'. And they were getting what they wanted.

The implicit censorship in sponsorship is rarely made so explicit, but in 1990 Terry Hands, announcing his retirement as Artistic Director of the RSC, spoke (on television) of sponsors who had told him: 'In future you will have to kowtow to us.' He later told me they said it 'in the nicest possible way', but it still sounds rather ominous to me. In 1991, Colin Tweedy, Director General of ABSA, confessed to being concerned to hear of sponsors making comments about the suitability of certain artistic productions. 'It is a very dangerous trend,' he admitted but strangely added, as if it were an excuse, 'in a recession businessmen will want far more quantifiable results'.

It is perhaps not very important that an RNT production of *'Tis Pity She's a Whore* failed to attract sponsorship because sponsors' consorts would not like to be associated with that rude word. It is more disturbing that the same theatre's production of David Hare's *Secret Rapture* also failed to attract sponsors because one of its leading characters was a somewhat Thatcherite lady who was not shown in a very favourable light. More seriously, the excellent Theatre Royal at Stratford East was refused sponsorship by a bank on the grounds that it had put on a play satirising Mrs Thatcher and her government. (This was, of course, before it became permissible to attack Mrs Thatcher.) Philip Hedley, the Director of Stratford East is a tough character who would never bow to a sponsor's censorship and he has subsequently won a handsome sponsorship award from Prudential.

In general, sponsors like to play safe. 'We would never sponsor anything way out,' said one, while another said his company preferred to sponsor art exhibitions 'with which it was comfortable'. This raises special problems when it comes to sponsoring theatre. A leading sponsor, Victor Head, published a good book in 1981 called *Sponsorship: the newest marketing skill* (a significant title), in which he noted that whilst sponsoring music is fairly safe, 'the stage, more than anything else in the arts, can arouse public controversy and controversy is usually bad for business'. He therefore judges that the theatre has a tough task in dispelling 'a sponsor's nightmare of seeing his company linked to some semi-pornographic assault on private enterprise', when he thought he was sponsoring something safe.

There are a few, very few, exceptions to this 'safety rule', one of the most conspicuous being Mobil's sponsorship of provocative new plays at the Royal Exchange Theatre, Manchester. In general, the sponsor's preference for safe art may be expected to continue – even in music, for Luke Rittner confessed that sponsored orchestras may be tempted to cut out Maxwell Davies in favour of Beethoven, and John Drummond has recalled his experience of sponsorship during his stint as director of the Edinburgh Festival:

'We put on the kind of concerts that wouldn't frighten directors' wives.' People in the sponsorship business admit that 'chairman's whims' are still too often a factor in determining what to sponsor. Michael Billington, the Guardian's respected theatre critic, warned a few years ago that advocates of sponsorship should consider its effects on the freedom of the artist. Arts Council money, he wrote, comes without strings, but a sponsor, while he is unlikely to quarrel over a season of classical rep, will threaten to withdraw the moment anything controversial raises its head. He concluded that no modern British play would have lasted long if it had had to depend on sponsorship. An obvious victim would have been *Look Back in Anger*, a milestone in post-war theatre, and we know that even the RSC's enormously successful dramatisation of *Nicholas Nickleby* failed to get sponsorship because it was considered 'too adventurous'. It is, of course, one of the prime functions of the arts to challenge accepted ideas, moral, political and religious – even to make us uncomfortable. It looks as though that function may have to be played down in the brave new world of increasingly sponsored arts.

Questioning public subsidy

We have seen that in 1979, the long and generally respected tradition of public subsidy was put on the back burner. When Lord Gowrie was appointed Arts Minister, I sent him a paper on developing wider access to the arts, which I imagined should be a prime concern of an arts minister. He did not acknowledge it and when I met him at my retirement party, I asked whether he had read it. 'Oh, yes', he replied, 'but my main concern is to foster the growth of business sponsorship'. By then, it had become fashionable for some Tories to attack the whole idea of public funding as leftish, although it had been inaugurated with all-party support.

The general ideology of the 1980s was (ironically) indicated by the speech of the minister responsible for social services, John Moore, when he told the 1987 Conservative Party Conference: 'Everyone knows the sullen apathy of dependence and can compare it with the sheer delight of personal achievement.' Sir William Rees-Mogg, then Chairman of the Arts Council agreed with Moore and applied his view to the arts, saying 'Of course John Moore is right that subsidy creates dependence'. He particularly thought the National Theatre depended too much on subsidy. This was at a time when government expenditure on arts subsidies, whether

measured as expenditure per head of population or as a percentage of gross national product was far below the level in European
countries like France, Germany or Scandinavia. It still is. Moreover, the subsidised arts return more to government in taxes than
they receive in subsidy, so that while some Tories tended to regard
subsidy as a kind of welfare dole, wiser judges saw it as a very
sound investment. In 1990, the Artistic Director of English National
Opera pointed out (*The Times*, 3 April 1992), the arts contributed
£6 billion to the British balance of payments, £2 billion more than
the motor industry.

I have never been able to understand why dependence on sponsorship which, as we have seen involves much more ingratiating
behaviour than applying for public subsidy, should be seen as brac-
ing. Indeed, Peter Hall described the process of getting it to me
as 'a kind of whoring'. Certainly, 'the delight of personal achievement' is to be found in artistic work itself, not in wooing sponsors.

Plural funding

Defenders of sponsorship invoke the virtues of plural funding – a
mixture of public subsidy and sponsorship – as a guarantee of
freedom in the arts. The argument is frequently heard, but the
most plausible form was that elaborated by Paul Channon, when he
was Arts Minister. He wound up his speech at the Royal Academy
Dinner in 1982 with a declaration of faith about arts funding: 'I
believe in a mixed economy. In the arts for the foreseeable future,
the public sector is likely to pay the lion's share. But the private
sector [i.e. business] has a crucial role to play. How dangerous it
would be, how impossible for the rebel, how wrong, if the state
were ever to become the sole supporter of the arts.'

Nine years later, the then Conservative Arts Minister, Timothy
Renton, echoed Channon's sentiments, confessing 'How tempted I
might be, if I alone paid the piper, to insist that I call the tune.'
He went on to say he would hate to see Harold Pinter hounded as
writers were under Stalin. In fact, Pinter developed his powers
and rose to fame at a time when theatres depended much more on
public subsidy than now. So did Alan Ayckbourn, who has expressed
his gratitude to the subsidised theatre that gave him the opportunity to learn his craft. Norman St John Stevas (as he then was)
was much wiser when he said that paradoxically, the more government funds the arts, the freer they are. Mr Renton failed to take
account of the difference between our free, democratic society and

the Stalinist dictatorship and also (ominously) ignored the fact that the subsidy system in this country has been universally admired precisely because government hands over funds to an independent organisation, the Arts Council, and does not itself make artistic judgements. Our system means (or used to mean) that politicians *indirectly* pay the piper and do not call the tune.

In any case, I know of no instance where "rebel" artists have found sponsors more sympathetic than the Arts Council. Indeed, in my ten years' association with the Council, it was regularly under attack from Conservative MPs for being too generous to rebels – especially in the theatre.

Promoting sponsorship

This has been a critical, but, I hope, fairly argued review of sponsorship. There is a great deal of publicity in favour of sponsorship and little public criticism. Arts world figures have said to me privately, after I have published articles on sponsorship: 'We're glad you're saying it. You will understand that we can't speak or write publicly about our difficulties with sponsorship.' After reading an article by me on sponsorship, the head of one of our most prestigious arts organisations wrote to me: 'You are right, of course, and when I sup with sponsors in future, I shall use a longer spoon; *but sup I must*' (and that is why I cannot name him).

ABSA's task of promoting the idea of sponsorship is very efficiently done. Its reports and other publications are beautifully (and expensively) designed and produced and the larger sponsors produce their own very handsome publicity for what they do. ABSA also arranges glamorous dinners and ceremonies and I should say that I have been invited to several and found them very enjoyable, even if I have often disagreed with some of the speeches. My presence at such occasions demonstrates the generous spirit of Colin Tweedy, ABSA's Director General. He knows my views and we have argued many times, but I respect him and think he has done an outstanding job at ABSA. He has, of course, worked with a strong and favourable wind of government policy behind him and must take comfort from the fact that Labour arts policy at the 1992 election included no proposals to curb sponsorship.

At the 1991 annual ABSA Awards ceremony, Tweedy told a packed National Theatre that the achievements of sponsorship are often unsung. In fact they are sung far more often and loudly than the greater achievements of public subsidy. The Awards ceremony

itself is a highly prestigious event, graced by royals and leading
figures from the arts world. The proceedings open with a specially
commissioned fanfare of trumpets and when they are over, the
large audience of people from the worlds of arts, business and
politics, including the Arts Minister, the Leader of the Opposition
and yours truly, are regaled with champagne and succulent finger
foods. (You might almost say that the sponsor-ship floats on a sea
of champagne.) These events were sponsored by the *Daily Telegraph*
(since replaced by *The Times*), and each member of the audience
was given a copy of the day's special issue, containing four pages
celebrating the glories of sponsorship.

These pages were written in ad-man's hyperbole. Introducing
them was a passage disarmingly admitting that altruism is not a
sponsor's main motive. Another article more crudely admitted that
by sponsoring, a company can 'plug its products and make money'.
It added that sponsorship 'is like advertising, but – if used properly
– much more effective'. This makes you sceptical of a major bank's
claim, on the same page, that its sponsorship was an exercise in
'corporate social responsibility'. The next day, there was generous
coverage of the awards, bringing commendation of sponsorship to
millions of readers.

In the nearly half a century of the existence of public subsidy
of the arts, it has never been given such high-powered publicity
for the simple reason that no one would dare use public money
for such a purpose and the most altruistic sponsor would not
dream of funding such an exercise. And yet, it is important that
taxpayers, as the source of public subsidy funds, should know
what is being done with their money. My ten years' experience at
the Arts Council was that most of them do not know. I found that
even MPs often had no idea that arts institutions they knew well
were subsidised by the Arts Council. That is why I insisted, against
much opposition, that Arts Council subsidy should be acknow-
ledged. Nevertheless, acknowledgement often does not appear or is
so tiny as to be almost invisible, unlike the sponsor's name, even
though they have contributed far less.

Politics and sponsorship

The boosting of sponsorship in the Thatcher years was associated
with a talking down of public subsidy, not just by right-wing Tory
MPs but by arts ministers themselves. In the 1987 general election

the Tory Party was the only one not to publish on arts policy, but immediately after the election, Richard Luce, re-appointed by Mrs Thatcher to become the longest serving arts minister, took a tougher line with the arts community than any of his predecessors. He told a conference of Regional Arts Associations that too many of them had yet to be weaned away from 'the welfare state mentality' which he defined (wrongly) as a belief that 'the taxpayer owes them a living' (echoes of John Moore). He told them not to complain about the low level of government funds for the arts, warning that opinion was in any case swinging against government funding. In fact, independent research, by the Policy Studies Institute, shows that two-thirds of the taxpayers favour public funding of the arts. Nevertheless, the following year, Luce told the same conference: 'Abandon preconceived ideas about arts funding and be ready to take new initiatives.' He made quite clear what he meant, saying 'Private [i.e. business] support is the engine for expansion in the arts. My vision for the millenium is for private patronage of the arts to match or even outstrip public patronage' (*The House Magazine*, 29 January 1990).

Bearing in mind the figures given at the beginning of this chapter, the realisation of Luce's vision would require either an enormous growth in sponsorship or a severe cut in public funding – or both. His vision, not disowned by his successors, goes well beyond that of ABSA which has always declared that its role is to supplement, not supplant public funding. Indeed, in the same year as Luce's announcement of his vision, Colin Tweedy was saying 'We don't want to do the government's job and it's their job to fund the arts.' As Britain's largest sponsor, Ian Rushton of Royal Insurance, declared that the government's commitment to the RSC had failed to keep pace with inflation and business and he was not prepared to let government slide out of its responsibility to be the prime funder of the arts. His warning was apparently more effective than the RSC's own pleading: Luce quite suddenly found more money for the arts – though far from enough to meet their needs. By the end of 1992, ten leading arts development officers were writing to *The Times* (18 December 1992) to warn that the arts were threatened by falling sponsorship and reduced government subsidy. There has been nothing to suggest that a Conservative government with a new mandate will not revert to its vision of invigorating sponsorship outstripping debilitating public subsidy, particularly after business confidence recovers from the effects of recession. It is a vision that could well prove a nightmare for the arts world, forcing it to depend increasingly on monies used 'primarily and exclusively for the purpose of trade'.

TONY COOK

Sponsorship and Sport

Sport creates an image. The very word conjures a picture in the mind. In the vast majority of cases the feeling engendered by that picture is positive.

One of the primary aims of marketing is to create a positive image of a product. This is achieved in a variety of ways. One of the most tried and trusted is to forge a mental association with a clean and healthy activity. Sport fits the bill.

The Olympic motto of swifter, higher, stronger promotes the notion of mankind stretching itself to its limits. It's the pursuit of human excellence for no other reason than excellence itself. Whilst the Olympics themselves may have political overtones, their code, which is the raison d'être of all sport, carries none.

Aleardo Buzzi of the Marlboro cigarette company said in *Newsweek* magazine in 1983 of his company's motor racing sponsorship: 'We are the number one brand in the world. What we wanted was to promote a particular image of adventure, of courage, of virility.'

Joe MacGregor of Saatchi and Saatchi Sponsorship puts it even more clearly: 'Sport permeates the lives of billions of people around the world and provides a company with a vehicle with which to position its whole image or identity whilst providing support programmes across many levels. Opportunities to Leverage Advertising, PR, Sales Promotion and Hospitality complete a very attractive and effective medium for many companies.'

It is often difficult to put into hard cash terms the effects of sponsorship but one example that can be traced directly is the £7 million put into the 1989/90 Whitbread Round the World Race by Lion Nathan Breweries of New Zealand. Their yacht, *Steinlager 2*, won the race and gained an estimated £35.3 million in free advertising around the globe. Sales of Steinlager went up by 24 per cent in the United States and 21 per cent internationally.

Of course not all sports are thus. Some are tainted by scandal. Athletics, for example, has suffered under the drug abuse scandal personified by Ben Johnson. Some are tainted by violence. Association Football internationally is not in the big earners league from sponsorship and one of the prime reasons is the crowd trouble in Britain and Europe over the past decade. Some are tainted by lack of public interest. Volleyball and basketball are major international sports but their lack of popularity in this country means that they must struggle to attract domestic cash.

The big earners internationally are golf, tennis and motor racing. Stephen Aris in his book *Sportsbiz* lists the top 20 sporting earners of 1989. He does not include prize money or nonsports related investment income. This is cash earned from sponsorship, endorsements, exhibitions and appearance fees. Incredibly at the top of the tree is golfer Arnold Palmer with $9 million. Next comes another golfer, Greg Norman, on $8 million. The list continues with Boris Becker, Jack Nicklaus, Ayrton Senna, Alain Prost, Nelson Piquet, the Englishmen Nigel Mansell and Nick Faldo, then the first woman, Steffi Graf, and on down with Bernhard Langer, Chris Evert, Ivan Lendl, Jackie Stewart, Curtis Strange, Lee Trevino, Sandy Lyle, the Japanese golfer Ayako Okamoto, Seve Ballesteros, and Martina Navratilova who pulls in a mere $2.46 million. Not a single player of the world's most popular game, football, amongst them.

The three sports dominate. All are played by individuals as opposed to teams. All have a clean cut image. They are truly international and therefore attract the mega-buck attention of the multinational companies.

These sports provide a company with a ready association with the best in life. They represent cleanliness, health, achievement, triumph over adversity, strength and bravery. The association between a product and a sporting event or individual transfers the excellence of one to the other. It provides the instant recognition of a brand name in the best possible setting. Think of Cornhill and the sports fan thinks of warm, balmy days watching the magic and mystery of a test match unfold. Graham Gooch is standing up to the might of the West Indian fast bowlers, Robin Smith is taking the Australian attack to the cleaners, Neil Fairbrother is bright and fast in the field. The mind is filled with the passion, the fury and the sheer pleasure of a wonderful day's cricket. If England sink to one of their customary debacles then Cornhill are not to blame. If the national side rises above its usual dismal state then Cornhill share in the glory. The link between sporting excellence and business excellence is made. The company's name becomes a household name and that all important aim of the marketing department, 'positive branding', is achieved.

Peter Lawson is the General Secretary of the Central Council for Physical Recreation (CCPR), the independent umbrella organisation for voluntary sporting bodies in Britain. He is also the secretary of the Institute of Sports Sponsors. Mr Lawson sees no problem in wearing both hats. 'It is very important for the governing bodies of sport to have good relations with commercial companies that sponsor sport because sponsorship is the most significant financial strength in sport. Without commercial sponsorship there wouldn't be sport as we know it today. Over £200 million per year goes in, that we can identify. Much more than that goes in to back up the sponsorship of certain companies. It's no good Barclays, for example, sponsoring the Football League competition, giving it around two and half million quid, unless they're prepared to support and back that investment. At Football League clubs every Saturday they'll have little hospitality units, they'll be taking important customers, they spend a lot which doesn't go directly to the sport but it all adds to the bill of Barclays. The Sports Council grant from the government to all of sport is 47 million quid so you can see how significant sponsorship is.'

Sports sponsorship takes various forms. These are divided by the CCPR into six categories:

1. Event specific, such as the Yonex All England Badminton Tournament or The Embassy World Professional Snooker Championships.
2. Individual specific, such as Pringle's clothing contract with Nick Faldo.
3. Team specific, such as Tottenham Hotspur FC with Holsten.
4. Competition specific, the Coca Cola Cup, the NatWest Trophy or Rugby Union's Courage Leagues.
5. Ground specific, the Fosters Oval.
6. Coaching Scheme specific, such as Esso in youth swimming or Dairy Crest in athletics.

It is inevitably important for a sponsor to identify which of these forms will suit its aims and objectives. Barclays, for example, participate in two very different forms of sponsorship. The bank is well-known for its funding of the Football League but it also has a £10 million annual budget for its Community programme. Not all of that cash goes into sport. £4 million goes to charity, £2 million to employment initiatives, but £700,000 goes into community sponsorship which takes in the arts and sport. Barclays sponsors twenty-five sports involving over sixty competitions through its involvement with the British Polytechnics Sports Association. It also sponsors the English Women's Hockey Association and a wide range of inter-schools tournaments in a variety of sports that involve more than five thousand teams each year. Barclays Public Relations Officer Pat Kilbane says that: 'It's all about putting into the community what we take out. It's not a hard sell and so we've never tested what, if any, business we may gain through it. It really is about being involved in the community and that's very important to us.'

Barclays' Chairman Sir John Quinton says in his message promoting the scheme: 'We prosper on community strength. We aim to ensure that the community continues to prosper on ours.'

The aim of their Football League sponsorship is very different. The money for that comes out of a separate budget, is run by a separate department and is very much a part of the bank's hard commercial outlook. The opportunities to present the name of Barclays to the public are enormous. Every time the football results are read on television or radio it's referred to as the 'Barclays Football League'. There are 2,000 games each season which gain regional, national and international exposure. The English Football League is seen on television in seventy different countries. Each of the ninety-three League clubs has formed a relationship, if not necessarily an account, with its local Barclays branch. Barclays get two promotion boards at each ground, one page in each programme and ten VIP tickets for each match. The bank also runs the Manager of the Month, Young Eagle of the Month and Performance of the Week awards which give an opportunity for sixteen presentations each month with the local bank manager seen on the pitch.

Barclays stepped into the breach with the Football League. In 1987 the *Today* newspaper pulled out of its sponsorship in midsummer leaving just a matter of weeks for the League to get a new name on its masthead. Barclays had just been overtaken as the country's number one bank by NatWest and was keen to restore itself to the top of the heap. It had also suffered badly in the student market over its policy towards South Africa and now wanted to recapture lost ground. Football seemed perfect. The original cost for a three year deal from the 1987/88 season was £4.55 million with a top fee payable each year starting at £1.3 million rising to £1.75 million. The bank renewed its sponsorship in the 1990/91 season for a blanket sum of £7 million and a top up rising from £2.2 million to £2.5 million in the season 1992/93. Barclays admit that they got a very good deal at first but their commitment to the value of the deal has been proven by the renewal. The bank also stress that they do not just lend their name to the game, it's a sponsorship they make work with their active involvement. The deal has also had an unforeseen knock-on effect amongst the bank's own staff. Barclays are convinced their involvement with the national game has given a new pride to their employees thereby boosting staff morale.

It isn't easy for any commercial company to quantify in hard cash terms the effects of sponsorship but Barclays know through active research that the deal has raised their profile and that automatically leads to an increase in business. The company has regained its position as the country's leading bank and it has increased its community involvement. The fact that Association Football is widely perceived as a badly run, money losing game doesn't seem to worry the Bank. The link doesn't appear to have been made by the footballing public who are more interested in points won, promotion and relegation than in the profitability of their local team.

Save and Prosper sponsor the Home Rugby Union championships. Their Sponsorship Manager, Simon Curtis, is very clear why they picked this particular tournament. 'Our target audience is the male ABC1 aged forty plus. We looked at the arts but they didn't deliver the goods in terms of a television audience and then we looked at sport. Hockey didn't have a large enough following. Cricket, we decided, was over sponsored and then we hit on Rugby Union. It had a perfect audience, it almost mirrored our customer base, and it was virtually unsponsored. We found that for not enormous money we could pick up the big events.' Save and Prosper have now been involved for seven years and have put in for two more. Over the nine years the company will have paid approximately three million pounds. 'Quite a bargain,' says Mr Curtis. He stresses that it's never possible to perfectly analyse the results of sponsorship. Save and Prosper do run a continuing corporate advertising campaign and, naturally, do research on its effectiveness. They have noticed that since they began their rugby sponsorship there has been a dramatic increase in their name awareness but Mr Curtis adds the rider that this coincided with a television advertising campaign.

'Inevitably it gets to people who hadn't thought of you before,' he says. 'There's an enormous affinity between the sponsors and the sponsored. As a cricketer my club go to Cornhill to insure our cricket pavilion and the same is true between Save and Prosper and rugby. It gives you a sporting chance that the customer will favour you over your competitors.'

One of the more surprising sports sponsorships in this country has been the involvement of the Japanese wine and spirits firm, Suntory, with golf's World Matchplay Championships held each

year at Wentworth. Jun Tanaka, their Manager of Corporate Development and Planning, explains that they were already involved
in golf, tennis and basketball in Japan when they heard that the
World Matchplay organisers were looking for new sponsors. 'We
wanted to do the greatest event in the world. The Japanese golfer,
Isao Aoki, had done very well the year before, he had even got a
hole-in-one, and so there were great hopes in Japan. We made the
condition that there must be live television of the event in Japan
even though it was in the middle of the night. We also insisted
that there must be at least one Japanese player in the tournament
each year. I think that's only fair as it helped sell the TV rights in
Japan.' Suntory kept up their sponsorship for twelve years and
found that it paid dividends, in Japan. In Britain the base for
marketing their goods has always been limited but where there is a
chance to do so they find an easy entry as people know their name.
Their main business over here is the distribution of beer and
whisky to Japanese clients. Golf, though, is such an international
sport that the sponsorship of an event half way around the world
from the main market has proved effective. Suntory has now pulled
out of the event. Mr Tanaka says: 'Twelve years is one cycle in
Japanese culture, it is a Zodiac cycle. Now we've switched to culture rather than sport. In Japan the range of people's hobbies is
very wide now, it used to be only sport. People's tastes are changing and we try to move ahead of the times.'

Perhaps the most risky form of sports sponsorship is with the
individual. When it goes well, it goes very well indeed but for every
hit there are a good many misses. Pringle of Scotland started to
sponsor Nick Faldo when he was just another prospect on the
European Tour. Their Managing Director Graham Hayward is
coy about revealing the exact terms of their relationship with the
golfer but it's clear that their financial success is now irrevocably
linked. Pringle sell the Nick Faldo Collection that is designed
purely for the growing golf market. Mr Faldo picks up a royalty
on each product sold and Pringle get their name across the television sets of the world as Faldo continues to grab the major hon-
ours. Mr Hayward admits: 'We've gone to the heights of international media coverage. We wouldn't be able to afford it in straight
advertising costs. It's tremendous coverage. It's cheap and prestigious advertising and if all goes well then we will all enjoy success,
but it is a gamble.'

For the governing bodies of sport, sponsorship has provided a
lifeline. Britain, the inventor of most of the world's great sports,

is the most taxed sports nation in the western world. Peter Lawson, in an article in the *Daily Telegraph*, states that in the year 1989/90 the government received from sport an estimated total of £2.5 billion in the form of VAT, Income and Corporation Tax and betting levies. In return the government grant to the Sports Council was £52 million in the same period. Mr Lawson concludes: 'How refreshing to record that against this background of doom, gloom and indifference, there shines the beacon of commercial sponsorship. Currently, more than a thousand companies subscribe more than £200 million to sport in various sponsorship schemes, thereby witnessing to their faith in the future of British sport. Left to government funding and without commercial sponsorship, sport in Britain could not survive.'

The major sports with their guaranteed television coverage have no difficulties in finding sponsors. It is the minor sports, the up and coming individual competitors and the youth schemes that have the problems.

Josie Grange is the Sponsorship and Promotions Manager for the Amateur Swimming Association. For many years swimming was one of the mainstays of televised sport but in recent times its popularity as a small screen spectacle has declined. The ASA now has to budget for survival with or without a sponsor. Without sponsorship certain events would not take place at all, doctors and physiotherapists would be unable to travel with teams, specialised food would be out of the question, facilities for swimmers, journalists and administrators would be severely reduced, development work with potential medallists would be curtailed and their national learn-to-swim scheme would probably not exist. Swimming gets a Sports Council grant of £150,000. It takes in between £150,000 and £200,000 per annum in sponsorship. A handful of individual swimmers get personal sponsorship but for most it's a desperate battle to make ends meet.

Basketball is an even more extreme case. It is a major international sport which attracts huge sums of money in most other countries. In Italy, for example, a Yugoslav player has recently been signed for a $16 million tax free contract, twice the sum paid by Napoli for the world's top footballer, Diego Maradona. Basketball has long been seen as ripe for development here but an early Channel Four experiment with regular weekly basketball was a flop. The attraction of a weekly televised spot brought in a sharp increase in cash. But when the television stopped, the sponsors fled and basketball has been struggling ever since. Kevin Routledge is the

Chairman of the Basketball League and the owner of the Leicester Riders team. He says that the League as a whole can get a sponsor but individual teams struggle. His side depends on city council support of less than six figures per annum. Leicester drew Zaragossa of Spain in the 1991/92 main European club competition, the Korac Cup. Zaragossa's annual budget is £2.5 million. Leicester Riders were beaten out of sight.

It's a case of Catch 22, basketball can't grow in this country until it can show to fans that it's of a reasonable quality. It can't do that until it can attract cash and it can't attract cash until it gets television coverage. Television isn't interested until there's substantial European success. In the 1990/91 season, against all the odds, Cadburys Boost Kingston did achieve some of that success and a degree of TV time but sadly it wasn't enough. The club moved to Guildford, the team broke up, the sponsors changed and the vicious circle was not broken.

It's the relationship between television time and a sport that determines that sport's attraction to sponsors. Josie Grange admits that the BBC's decision on whether or not to show a particular swimming event on a particular Saturday afternoon makes all the difference. Even then swimming cannot capitalise completely as it will be shown in a multi-sport programme like *Grandstand* and cannot guarantee how many minutes it will receive. The 1991 national championships were sponsored by Optrex who came in at the last minute for £10,000. A number of other sports events were cancelled that afternoon due to the weather and the BBC ended up showing more swimming than originally planned. Optrex got a great deal.

Joe MacGregor of Saatchi's puts the case from the other side: 'In general terms, media exposure is still the most important criteria for a sponsorship and with television continuing to devote extensive air-time to sports programming, sport with its wide ranging reach and appeal provides the most cost effective marketing vehicle for a sponsoring company.'

There is an agreed code of conduct between television and sport over sponsorship. It basically boils down to two advertising banners, a verbal mention of the sponsor's name in the introduction and a written mention in the *TV* or *Radio Times*. But the deal is not all one way. There is no direct payment from a sponsor to a television company but the sponsor's cash is as vital to the TV stations as it is to sport. Peter Lawson explains: 'At the end of the day the BBC and ITV need a sponsor for sports events. They can't pay for themselves. If, for example, the BBC wants to cover League Football then the League will say we want four and a half million quid a year out of you. The BBC scream 'we can't do that' so the Football League say to Barclays Bank, you give us two and a half million and you can have your name up, now TV, you can do it for two million. It makes it possible to get on the screen, it's of mutual interest. Without a doubt sponsored sport is cheap telly.'

Steven Barnett in his book *Games and Sets: the Changing Face of Sport on Television* gives a classic illustration of this theory with the negotiations for television coverage of football in 1983. At the time ITV and the BBC negotiated a joint agreement. In March their final offer of £2.6 million was rejected by the Football League chairmen and for a while it seemed that league soccer would not be seen on the nation's screens. The main sticking point had been shirt advertising. The television companies refused to allow it and the clubs wanted more money in compensation for that ban. There existed the potential for up to a million pounds coming into the game if the television companies would allow a name on a shirt and the clubs wanted the cash. In the end television relented. In July shirt advertising was deemed to be acceptable so long as the logo did not exceed sixteen square inches and the sponsor's name was no more than two inches high. In return television was allowed to show, live, ten league games a season and the League Cup Final. The deal struck was worth exactly the same amount as that rejected in March, £2.6 million.

The cross-over between the media and the sponsors is getting greater. It is becoming more and more common for a sponsor to provide a journalist to cover an event. One of the first people to appreciate this new market was Tony Delahunty. 'What I try to do is bridge the gap between the sponsored tournament and the media coverage of it. That's a very difficult thing to do. At the one end there's the marketing genius with his seven degrees and all the jargon in the world, at the other is the hard bitten journalist who, certainly up to a few years ago, liked nothing better than to strike the sponsor's name out of any copy.'

Tony Delahunty Associates believe they offer a genuine service to both media outlets and sponsors. He says he is prepared to ditch a client if they make unreasonable demands for name plugs and quotes a story of a motoring event a couple of years ago. TDA prepared a three and a half minute preview tape of the event to send round to radio stations. In it was one mention of the sponsor as part of the name of the event. The sponsor's name was also mentioned in the cue, the piece read out by the presenter leading up to the piece. This could, of course, be removed by the radio station. The tape was sent off to the client's public relations company. They demanded six mentions of the sponsor's name in the piece, Delahunty refused, waived the fee and lost the client.

'It's a matter of trust. I have built up a relationship with a good many radio stations and if I begin to send out rubbish with obvious plugs then my good name goes down the pan. My credibility and professionalism are on the line and so I must say 'No' to a sponsor who makes unreasonable demands.'

Delahunty also stresses the standard of his reporters. Rod Whiting covered the Volvo European Tour in 1990 for a large number of radio stations all over the world. At one event, the Benson and Hedges Masters at St Mellion, there were a number of complaints from the golfers about the timing of the event. It was played in freezing cold conditions and the course was therefore not at its best. Whiting sent out actuality of the golfers complaining. Delahunty admits: 'My reporters are there to report the sport. They don't go looking for problems but it's an important part of my contract that my people will cover the event as is.'

His business has expanded in the recession. There are more media outlets around with fewer resources and they all want their "own" reporter at sports events. Sponsors can no longer afford to pay for large numbers of journalists to attend and so Tony Delahunty Associates provides the toothpaste in the financial squeeze. He provides pictures for television, sound for radio and copy for newspapers and the business is growing.

The delicate balance between the media, sport and sponsors is always going to be difficult. The Howell Committee of Enquiry into Sports Sponsorship in 1983 outlined many of the problems. Most of those problems still exist today. Howell found that many sports lacked expertise in dealing with the media, that some sponsors tried to squeeze more publicity from the media than was fair or realistic and that certain sections of the media gave greater prominence to critical news which made some in sport believe that no news was better than bad news. None of this is particularly surprising but the tripartite relationship is the key to continued sponsorship.

Television was perceived by the sporting bodies and sponsors interviewed by Howell to be the prime media target. Television itself told Howell it had a threefold responsibility. To present the best sport possible, to give adequate coverage to minority sport and to recognise that a great deal of sport would not take place without sponsorship and therefore to give a fair reflection of such assistance within the guide-lines already established.

The committee chose to agree with this and stressed its commitment to journalistic integrity. But, and in any committee report the 'but' always carries the sting, Howell goes on: 'Whilst we have already made it clear that TV does not exist for the convenience of sport, the antithesis of this proposition in our view also must be self-evident, for sport and television are very much dependent on each other.' That really is the nub of the argument. Sponsorship plays a part in a far larger relationship. That part continues to grow but it relies on the continuation of the balance being maintained between the other two sides and that balance, finally, is sustained by the public's continuing fascination with sport.

Howell also pointed out one of the prime problems in the whole complex deal, the role of the super agent. The most well-known of these, but by no means the only one operating, is Mark McCormack's International Management Group (IMG). In his evidence to the committee, Philippe Chartrier, then President of the International Tennis Federation, reported that Mr McCormack had said to him: 'You run your sport and I will do my business deals.' M. Chartrier went on: 'What happens is that sport allows him to find their money via sponsorship – this is the soft option – and then find he is gradually taking control.'

One of the most controversial of IMG's involvements has been with Golf's World Matchplay Championship. Senior Vice President Ian Todd told Howell: 'Without McCormack there would be no World Matchplay Golf Championship.' That was in 1982 but the row has not been resolved today. In 1991 José Maria Olazabal, then the number two golfer in the world, did not receive an invitation to the event. He was very angry: 'They should call it the International Management Group invitation, not the World Matchplay Championship.' Olazabal, who had turned down an invitation in 1990 because he wanted to concentrate on winning the European Order of Merit, told reporters he had rejected a number of offers to join the IMG stable, eight of whom formed the bulk of the twelve starters that year at Wentworth. However, Olazabal did play in 1992, but who will be next?

Howell was keen to build in safeguards against any such real or perceived conflict of interests but little has been done in the interim. The committee stated: 'It seems to us most undesirable that an organisation should be able to represent a governing body, sponsors, a significant number of top players, negotiate television, cable and satellite contracts and sell merchandising rights. The situation is pregnant with conflict of interests and cannot carry public confidence.' What Howell failed to add was that McCormack even formed part of the television commentary team!

For the individual sportsman or woman sponsorship is often vital. In the increasingly competitive world of international sport young British stars come up against opponents who have had the benefit of comparatively huge government backing. The German government, for example, spends £20 per person per annum on sport. The Italian government spends £5, the Danish £3. The British government spends 97 pence and taxes sport to a far greater extent than any of its comparable neighbours. The British Olympic Association, which receives no government assistance, was obliged to pay £750,000 tax on the £5 million brought in by fund raising to send competitors to the 1988 Games in Seoul. British facilities are also the worst in Europe and our youngsters must make do as best they can.

This government reluctance to support the nation's sporting excellence leaves any young man or woman who believes they have a chance of "making it" on the international stage with one option. They must train full time or they will not be able to compete with the foreign opposition. They must have the best facilities and the best coaches available or again they will be left behind in the international arena. They must find a sponsor.

For the companies this is the hardest form of sponsorship to grasp. It requires a bold move to promote, at considerable cost, a youngster with potential. The company can only hope that their pick will make it to the very top of the tree but that's an enormous gamble. Pringle's have done very well with Nick Faldo but for every Faldo there are hundreds of young golfers who never even get a card for the European Tour, let alone go on to win a string of major tournaments.

John Watson-Miller is an off-road motorcyclist. His aim is to become the first Briton on a motorcycle to complete the toughest rally in the world, the Paris-Dakar (in 1992 the Paris-Cape Town). He has already taken part in a number of smaller rallies, relying on small sponsors and his own cash. He just failed in his dream in 1991 when a broken foot and a set of smashed ligaments forced him to retire just a few days away from Dakar. For that attempt he had cash and backing from Honda and Camel. In 1992 he hoped to try again but it all depended on raising the cash. 'I see sponsorship as a means to an end. It is not a necessary evil, as my sport has changed. It is no longer just a sport, it's an advertising vehicle. Having said that, there are knock-ons for the sport as it become better-known through its use by advertisers. It's a symbiotic relationship. You can't compete without money and for 1992 I needed £70,000 to enter the Paris-Capetown. I accept that when I make a deal with a sponsor I enter into a business contract. I must promote the sponsor's product in every way I can. I will mention their name in TV and radio interviews, I will wear their goods and show the badges in photographs and I will make myself generally available to them.' Despite all that, John failed to raise the cash and didn't compete.

A straight comparison between two individuals can be made in the sport of swimming. James Parrack was number three in the world at the end of 1990. He had won a silver medal at the Commonwealth Games. He was no longer in the "potential" category, he had proved himself at the top and he needed cash to take that small step to the very top. Today he is still on the dole and his only assistance from the world of commerce is a car complete with its tax, insurance and servicing provided by the Eagle Star Insurance company.

Sharon Davies stormed to fame at the age of 14 when she won a European bronze medal in 1977. She went on to collect two Commonwealth Golds in 1978 and Olympic Silver in 1980. She retired but has since decided to return to swimming and won a silver and a bronze in the Commonwealth Games of 1990. Sharon has a major sponsorship from the sports drink firm, Dexters, and a car provided by Budget.

Sharon believes the Amateur Swimming Association doesn't do enough to market itself. She sees what Andy Norman has done for athletics and she wants swimming to follow suit. There are a number of top swimmers in this country who are articulate, attractive and capable of doing a great deal to promote the sport but until they become Gold Medallists they don't get the support from industry and commerce that they need. Compare the relative fortunes of Adrian Moorhouse and Nick Gillingham. Adrian won Olympic Gold by one hundredth of a second. He has been relatively well off ever since. Nick was pipped for the Gold by five hundredths of a second. He continues to struggle.

Sharon Davies was sponsored from the age of 15 through the efforts of her father. He tramped the country looking for backers and came up with £25,000 from Wimpey Construction and Konica.

LIBRARY , UNIVERSITY COLLEGE CHESTER

The Amateur Swimming Association at the time forbade individual sponsorship and so that cash had to be spread amongst the whole 16-strong British squad. Since then the ASA has changed its attitude but Sharon believes the progress is too slow. She also wants to see more swimmers actively going out to get in cash. 'You need to promote yourself and put a package together. It's a business. Any athlete must give a company a return whether it be through speeches, wearing insignia or openings of one sort or another. You must be available to give the company something back.'

She says that sponsorship has made her life a great deal easier. She can go and train without having to panic about where her next job will come from or about paying the bills. She was able to train in Portsmouth four days a week in the lead up to the Barcelona Olympics, staying in a decent hotel room, with the right coaches and the right facilities and no major financial worries. Yet, realistically, she had little chance of a medal. Compare her situation with that of James Parrack, less well-known, but a genuine prospect.

James, like Sharon, is a highly articulate, well educated and attractive personality. He has suffered to a certain extent from living in the shadow of Adrian Moorhouse but the two are neck and neck in training and James has age on his side. In 1987 he took a year out from Polytechnic to train and signed on the dole. He completed his studies in the next year, but since September 1989 he has relied on social security and his parents' generosity to pay his food and rent bills. He'll occasionally pick up a small amount of cash from a swimming club or the Olympic Schools Appeal for a personal appearance. He shares a house in Leeds with Adrian Moorhouse as the facilities in his home town of Cheltenham aren't good enough for his level of training. He struggles on and prays for Gold. James thinks a lot more could be done by companies at local level: 'I only want at most £10,000 a year and my life would be so much simpler. I could go to training camps abroad when I need to and I could enter competitions on mainland Europe where I would get good opposition but at the moment that's impossible.' He's tried every company with Leeds in its name but has met with a total blank. 'I accept that a company needs a return, but companies could get a lot more mileage out of sponsorship if they put their minds to it, especially on a local level. There's a lot of interest in swimming in Leeds and I could help take the name out to a lot more people.'

As it is, Parrack, like many other British competitors, has to compete with the ever present worries about money hanging over his head. He looks at his contemporaries in Canada and Australia with envy. They get a state grant each year determined by their international ranking. Once they make the top 50 they are guaranteed a certain amount of cash and that increases with each step up the ladder. 'If I was in Canada I would be given around £8,000 a year and that would make all the difference to me. It would mean I could definitely carry on without worrying all the time about money.'

Nick Brown was one of the key members of the British Davis Cup tennis squad. In 1991 he scored a spectacular first round victory at Wimbledon over one of the favourites, Goran Ivanisevic. He also played in the Davis Cup doubles with Jeremy Bates against Austria and secured a famous victory to take Britain back into the World Group. In 1984 Nick Brown gave up full-time competitive tennis because he could not find a sponsor. Instead he became a coach in France, Belgium and the privately run David Lloyd Tennis Centre at Heston, near Heathrow. It was a simple decision for Nick. He was ranked at 320 in the world at singles and at 140 in doubles. He had to travel the world to play in tournaments but could never make enough cash to finance himself. In 1989 he was persuaded by a number of businessmen amongst his trainees to return to the big time. Each of them put in £2,500 and in return they were to get back a percentage of his prize money and appearance fees. Nick admits: 'It was all a huge gamble.' Those private investors got around half their money back.

The next year L and R Engineering paid him to wear a patch, Head Racquets gave him equipment, Mazuno provided clothes and shoes and the Leeds-based computer firm, Holding, gave him some cash and a car. Nick Brown finished 1990 with a world ranking of 269 in singles and 43 in doubles. At long last he could make money in doubles tournaments. He made around $70,000 in winnings plus Davis Cup fees. Out of that came £10,000 in air fares and much the same again in hotel bills and living expenses. Nick admits: 'It's a hard way to make a living but in the last three years I wouldn't have swapped it for anything.' Ultimately though, those years away from international competition and practice took their toll and he has retired again.

Tennis, though, with the huge annual cash windfall from Wimbledon is changing. A number of tournaments for up and coming youngsters are sponsored by Volkswagen. Cellnet and Laings help with youth squads and the vital step up from promising youngster to world star is being made more possible.

There is the additional worry for all sporting bodies and indiv-

iduals about the quality of a sponsor. Some will make unreasonable demands in terms of what they expect in return and the relationship between the two sides can become brittle. Others will be
promoting a product that will be unacceptable to an individual.
Bernhard Langer, for example, will have nothing to do with any
alcohol related sponsorship. Although he was a member of the
Johnnie Walker Ryder Cup Team in 1991 he refused to allow his
name to be mentioned alongside the whisky in any shape or form.
But it isn't alcohol that causes most sports people to be on their
guard, it's tobacco.

There is no law against tobacco. It is a legal substance which
provides a great deal of revenue for the government. Peter Lawson,
representing the combined governing bodies of sport, says: 'One
of the great things about sports sponsorship in this country is that
it's not compulsory. No governing body has to take it and no
commercial company has to give it. Smoking is a legal entity. The
government is very happy to fund half the National Health Service
because of the revenue it gets from tobacco. The government is
very relaxed about it. Now we say this, and it's a question of freedom. If a governing body decides that there is no damage done to
their sport by taking tobacco money they should be free to do so
if they're lucky enough to get it. A number of sports will not
touch it. They won't touch it not because they have a particular
hang-up about tobacco but because, and let's take swimmers as an
example, in the main the top swimmers are youngsters and it
would look wrong to be alongside it. Gymnasts are the same and
athletes are the same. But bowls and darts and snooker, there are
no image problems there and there's no conflict of any kind whatever. What is more the CCPR believes, and I'm sure they're right,
that people do not, having clapped their eyes on a motorcar bearing a fag sign, rush off and buy a packet of fags. People are much
more sophisticated than that. So our view is that the list of products that the do-gooders, the latter-day puritans, will proclaim bad
for us is endless. If something's illegal and the government declare
it so then we won't touch it. If not, will people please clear off and
let us make our own decisions?'

It is difficult to quote an exact figure for the amount of tobacco
sponsorship of sport but the most reliable figure would seem to be
the Tobacco Advisory Council's three per cent which equates to
around £5 million per annum. It is significant, though, that virtually every event which is tobacco-sponsored appears on television.
The latest figures available state that 364 hours of sport coverage

in 1989 were tobacco sponsored. That amount of advertising time would cost at least ten times the total sponsorship bill.

ITV has banned all tobacco-sponsored sport. The BBC says it is 'constantly vigilant' and 'rejects any suggestion that it is encouraging children to smoke'. In 1991 the BBC declined to show footage of the Monte Carlo Rally in *Grandstand* because one car was competing with the Marlboro logo clearly visible on the bodywork and the corporation felt that that was in breach of the voluntary agreement with the tobacco companies. The slot left vacant was filled with additional coverage of snooker sponsored by Benson and Hedges.

Action on Smoking and Health (ASH) is a charity set up by the Royal College of Physicians in 1971 to alert the public to the dangers of smoking. It argues a very different case to Mr Lawson's. The pressure group starts from the premise that sponsorship is another word for advertising and that by getting advertising space on television the tobacco companies are doing something that is banned by law. To back up their claim ASH quotes a survey of November 1989 which indicates that 64 per cent of children aged between 15 and 16 thought that cigarettes were advertised on TV.

ASH argues that the most significant effect of tobacco sponsorship of sporting events is to associate a uniquely dangerous and deadly product with success. Mark Flanagan, Deputy Director of ASH, says: 'The most important impact of a ban on tobacco sponsorship would be to finally disassociate sport from a product that kills 110,000 people in the UK each year.'

The Tobacco Advisory Council, the trade association of the UK tobacco manufacturers, take a different line. They claim in their magazine *Tobacco Matters*: 'Were tobacco sponsorship to be banned, many sports – including grassroots events – would struggle to survive. In recent years over sixty sports – as diverse as fly-fishing, golf, snooker, rugby league, show jumping and amateur tennis – have benefited from tobacco sponsorship.'

That response is countered by Mark Flanagan: 'If any ban came into force it would be through an EEC directive. That would be effective from 1995 at the earliest and I am sure that there would be no difficulty in finding new sponsors for high profile events by then.' He is also hopeful of the role to be played by the newly set up Foundation for Sport and the Arts which is funded by the pools companies to the tune of £60 million per annum. He believes the Foundation could either offer to help organisations and events ready to collapse due to a loss of sponsorship or set up special consultancies and study groups to get new sponsors.

There are a number of quotes to back up his point of view:

> 'If we had to replace tobacco sponsors, we believe we could do so...'
> David Harrison, Chief Executive, World Professional Billiards and
> Snooker Association (*Yorkshire Post,* 17 May 1991)

> 'We get a number of enquiries asking when a contract comes to an end.
> I expect we would be able to sell the Benson and Hedges again to a new
> sponsor.'
> Peter Smith, Test and County Cricket Board
> (*Yorkshire Post,* 17 May 1991).

Ben Welsh is the Public Affairs Executive of the Tobacco Advisory
Council. He counters the ASH argument in a number of ways.
He says that tobacco being a unique product in its ability to kill is
only a matter of opinion: 'The individual has access to lots of
information and can make up his or her own mind. We're fed up
with the busybody classes always talking abut what people should
and shouldn't do.' This is not a view shared by any medical opinion. He does not oppose the right of every sport to make up its own
mind on tobacco sponsorship and agrees with what he describes as
the 'very tough' guidelines. He points out that tobacco is known
as a 'good sponsor' and, he claims, has saved some sports from
extinction. 'If tobacco hadn't sponsored cricket in the sixties then
cricket would be dead.' Mr Welsh disputes the claim that tobacco
sponsors will be easy to replace. Tobacco money is concentrated in
a relatively small number of sports and it provides a high percentage of those sport's income. He also points up the unchallenged
assertion that tobacco sponsorship is of a good quality: 'Tobacco
won't be easy to replace, especially not with sponsorship as loyal
and professional as tobacco has been.'

Sports sponsorship by the tobacco industry, though, has not
been banned by the EC and the British Government was instru-
mental in that. The last Minister for Sport, Robert Atkins, told me
in a 1990 interview on London Talkback Radio his views on tobacco and sport and since then there is no reason to suspect that
the government has changed its mind in any way: 'I'm a smoker
and I'm a drinker. I don't think the members of the British public
in the average pub or club are actively influenced by seeing Benson
and Hedges or Rothmans or Johnnie Walker. I don't think they go
out and spend an enormous amount of money getting drunk or
smoking themselves to death as a result of that. I have no aversion
to tobacco or alcohol sponsoring sport. I have enough faith in the
British public to think that they can make their own decisions on

what they smoke or drink according to their own views.'

The Conservative government's attitude to sport is a reflection of the government's overall social policy. If it is possible for the private sector to do it, then let it. The cash spent directly on sport by the government in 1990/91 was £43.7 million via the Sports Council and £670,000 via the Football Licensing Authority. In addition local authorities in England spent £389 million on current expenditure and £243 million on capital expenditure on sport. Urban Programme cash and City Challenge money add almost £20 million more, most of which is used to "prime the pump" to encourage private sector involvement. That adds up to £696.4 million in a year. The government took in £2.5 billion in revenue from sport in that same year.

The government does not believe that it could, or should, fund the whole of sport. It sees its role as one of providing the means to attract more private cash into the sector. The Department of National Heritage quotes its principal objectives in the field of sport as:

- Promoting participation by adults and young people, including those with disabilities, in sport and active recreation, encouraging and supporting as appropriate the provision of facilities.
- Encouraging all participants to better their own performance, and enabling champions to develop.
- Encouraging the rationalisation of sport administration in the UK.
- Enhancing the place of UK sport internationally.

There is no longer a Sports Minister. The Minister with responsibility for sport, along with numerous other portfolios, is Robert Key. It had been thought that the appointment of David Mellor as National Heritage Minister would do well for sport, and so it seemed, but his departure from the Cabinet was swift and his plans bore little fruit.

One major government innovation of late has been the Sportsmatch scheme. Under the deal local sport can gain up to £75,000 per project from the Department of National Heritage if the same amount is secured in business sponsorship. It concentrates on local amateur sport and is prepared to spend up to £3 million a year. It hardly compares with the revenue taken out of sport by the government.

And herein lies the rub. Sponsorship in sport cannot be seen in isolation. It is a part of the whole funding mix. At the moment, in Britain, it is the major part. That is true at every level except at school and even that is changing. The days of the old Olympian purist are long dead and buried. There is no such thing as truly amateur sport. It is also correct to say that no sponsorship is entirely for the benefit of sport. It is a two way process and the kudos, advertising, hospitality and image enhancement for the sponsor are always there to a greater or lesser extent. But is that necessarily a "bad thing"?

There is no doubt that the income derived from commerce and industry has provided huge benefit. Facilities have improved, standards have risen and more and more people are taking advantage of what sport has to offer. In comparison with our European partners, though, we still lag far behind on virtually every count in virtually every sport.

The missing link is government finance. The key to understanding the destitute state of so many of our sporting bodies is the revenue the government relies upon from sport. The flow is one way and the wrong way. It cannot be right in a country that is said to care for the health, leisure and well-being of its citizens that the government makes a huge net tax gain from sport.

That having been said, British industry and commerce should take a bow. The overall quality of British sponsorship is exceptional. Compare it with the experience of the United States of America, where it is now accepted that if a sponsor demands a change in the rules then a change in the rules will follow. The British sporting public would not accept such shenanigans. It is the passion of sports' participants and spectators in this country that has given the administrators the power to resist any possible demands from the advertisers. However, it must be stressed, there is very little evidence to demonstrate that domestic sponsorship has been a harmful influence and much to show its benefit. The international mega-agency is still a major worry but sports administrators are a lot sharper than they were. If they let in the big boys then they know what to expect.

The thorny question of tobacco sponsorship remains unresolved. Support for the moral arguments of either side depend on your overall view of life, your political morality. If you believe that freedom of choice includes charitable status for private schools, support for the private health industry and an acceptance that the weakest will go to the wall then it is likely that you will be happy with the present arrangements. If, on the other hand, you believe that private health damages the National Health Service, that a two-tier system of education is harmful and divisive and that government should intervene in the planning of the economy, then you are likely to favour a ban on tobacco sponsorship of sport. The debate is reminiscent of that on compulsory wearing of seat belts in cars or the enforced wearing of crash helmets on motor cycles. Finally, those who supported the argument for health and safety defeated those who defended 'freedom of choice'. Once the battle was over there was very little outcry.

The same will happen with tobacco sponsorship. It seems inevitable that eventually the EC will ban it and the British Government may even change political complexion and support such a move. There will, undoubtedly, be a great deal of yelling and screaming on the way but sport will find new sponsors and, in the long run, no one will miss the tobacco companies. A few competitions may disappear but whole sports will not go under.

It is high time there was a major government inquiry into the funding of sport in Britain. That inquiry should be given the remit of examining the income and expenditure of sport. It should compare our experience with that of our European partners, Australia, Canada and the United States, and it should compare the domestic funding of the arts with that of sport.

Sponsorship and advertising revenue should be the jam on the slice. At the moment they are the bread and butter. It is not fair on the sponsor, the advertiser, the participant, the spectator or the administrator. It's time the government recognised its responsibilities to the people of Britain. The only way that will be achieved is when the sporting bodies and the sporting public start to use their political clout. The reason we are poorly served in this respect by our elected rulers is because we have not chosen to exercise our political muscle for the good of sport, and until we do little will change. It could even be that the sponsors will join in such a crusade and then even a Conservative government may listen.

FRANCIS BECKETT

Sponsorship in Education

Great chunks of Britain's education system have been handed over to private enterprise to manage, control and even own. Successive Conservative Education Secretaries have expressed gratitude to 'public-spirited businessmen' who sponsor education.

But no company sponsors anything unless it expects to get something out of it. Generally, what it hopes for is a public relations advantage which, in the long or short term, will be reflected in sales. In education, it is not always as simple as that.

Schools and colleges can offer a more attractive target audience than any other sort of institution. A company would have to spend many millions of pounds to target, say, 11-year-olds, or first year degree students, in any other way than by buying an "in" to their schools or colleges.

There are many good reasons for targetting them. Companies want children to buy their products. They want children to influence the buying habits of parents. Sometimes companies are thinking long term, and want children to get into the habit of being well-disposed towards their products, which may affect their purchasing decisions when they grow up.

Sometimes, the sales advantage is at most a secondary objective. Companies are thinking of their future recruitment needs. They want children to grow up well-disposed towards the idea of working for the company. And they want children taught in such a way that they will be useful to the company. They know what sort of person they want to employ, and they want schools to produce that sort of person.

In higher education, sponsorship is often closely related to recruitment – even in periods of high graduate unemployment. Companies which recruit graduates like to think they are getting the best. So they try to persuade graduates to compete for a limited number of graduate jobs. Personnel departments are told to get 'the top five per cent' – though no one has ever worked out what this means.

Achieving the profile which will get graduates to regard working for your company as especially prestigious or rewarding is a delicate public relations task.

Higher education sponsorship is also attractive as a means of persuading higher education institutions to concentrate on those areas of study which are most useful to the sponsoring company.

Sponsored chairs and sponsored research do not come without strings.

In the Thatcher years, it became much easier for companies to do all these things. The government rushed to give the business community as much access to, and control of, the education system as it could want.

Education is being, in a real sense, privatised. The number of children in private schools increased from 5.7 per cent to 7.3 per cent between 1979 and 1991 (when it started going down again because of the recession). Conventional wisdom in middle-class areas now is that if you want a good education for your children, you have to pay.

At the same time, a great deal of what is supposed to be the maintained education system is being handed over to business people, to run in the same way that they run their businesses.

But business, to the government's surprise and disappointment, does not want to spend a lot of time and money educating Britain's children and young people. The more thoughtful business leaders have become thoroughly alarmed, and either begged the government for a smaller portion, or simply voted with their feet and stayed out of the government schemes.

Many companies have active community affairs departments and are members of the per cent club, which means that they put into community affairs at least a half of one per cent of pre-tax profits. But these companies have declined the government's pressing invitation to take over the education system. They think education is the government's job.

So the government has found itself paying huge sums of money to create links between education and business, in order to attract much smaller sums from private industry. It has used taxpayers' money in order to give big business something for relatively nothing.

Companies which take the money are generally the ones which claim that they can show feather-bedded public sector educationalists how things are done in 'the real world'. They are now in the ironic position of running schemes which are feather-bedded by public money.

That is fine for big businesses. Companies can have their cake, eat it, and then pretend it never existed in the first place. They can have their sales advantages and influence the curriculum; they can get the public relations advantage of being thought to be philanthropically contributing to education; and they can get all this for a bargain basement price.

It is less fine for schoolchildren and students, and for teachers and parents. They are being called on to pay, through their taxes, for big companies to run their sales pitches and their recruitment drives.

This policy is seen in its purest form in the City Technology Colleges.

City Technology Colleges

In October 1986 the then Education Secretary, Kenneth Baker, announced a 'pilot network of 20 City Technology Colleges (CTCs) in urban areas' and called for 'potential sponsors in the business community, the churches and existing educational trusts'.

CTCs were to be schools for 11-18 year olds 'providing free education with a bias towards science and technology'. The sponsors would be expected to 'meet all, or most, of the costs of buildings and equipment for the CTCs'. They would own, or lease, the CTCs, and run them. They would employ all teachers, and all other staff. The government would pay the CTCs' running costs.

'Pupils,' said Mr Baker, 'will span the full range of ability and be drawn from a substantial catchment area.' In other words, they were to be non-selective. But this was not quite true. Hardly drawing breath, the Secretary of State went on: 'They will be selected on the basis of their aptitude, their readiness to take advantage of the type of education offered in CTCs and their parents' commitment to full time educational training up to the age of 18 and to the CTC curriculum and ethos.'

What that has meant in practice is that CTCs to a great extent choose the children they think will be easy or rewarding to teach, and whose parents seem likely to co-operate and not make waves.

Mr Baker was quite happy, he told businessmen, for companies to name their CTCs after themselves.

CTCs, in other words, were to be the ultimate sponsorship opportunity. A business which sponsored a CTC would have its name engraved on the hearts of the pupils and parents; it would be known as a philanthropic company which valued education; and, by influencing the teaching, it would ensure that its future staff were getting an education designed to make them valuable to the company.

Mr Baker created a CTC Trust, headed by a businessman, Mr Cyril Taylor. Mr Taylor told the *Times Educational Supplement* that he had 'no objection to the monument principle' and would be delighted, if he got the chance, to promote, say, the Tesco CTC.

'Employers are telling me that the schools do not teach the skills that they require. In the CTCs that they fund, they will ensure that the correct skills are taught.'

I was shown round the first CTC, Kingshurst, near Birmingham, by David Wright, community affairs manager for GKN, the West Midlands based automotive company which is one of Kingshurst's sponsors. The spacious classrooms, stuffed full of the latest in communications technology, would have turned a teacher in most state schools green with envy. The brochure was the glossiest and most expensive I have seen.

Nearby, catering for the majority of the local population for whom there are no places at Kingshurst, are decaying, cash-starved schools.

Mr Wright explained that the bottom line for GKN sponsorship is that it must tangibly benefit the company. Seated in one of the classrooms, he showed me a GKN promotional video illustrating the wide variety of products GKN sells.

Then he introduced me to the GKN manager whom the company seconded to work in the school. This man, who has no previous educational experience, advises the head teacher and the staff about teaching and curriculum matters. His work alone must have made GKN's contribution to the school a good investment.

So CTCs seemed a wonderful deal for the sponsoring company. Yet getting sponsors to put in the huge sums expected proved impossible. The government quickly started offering CTCs at cut rates, with the taxpayer making up the rest.

The sponsor was no longer expected to meet 'all or most of the costs of building and equipment'. The target of £8-10 million in sponsorship money per CTC was quietly junked.

The government would accept £2 million, or one fifth of the cost, and be jolly grateful. It would happily put in about £10 million out of its overstretched education budget in return.

If it had not changed tack, there would be no CTCs. It required a lot of creative accounting just to make it look as though sponsorship had reached even the new, reduced figure.

In Lewisham, south London, for example, the government counted in the inflated value it attached to the school building. This building was 'given' by the Haberdashers Company, which was already running a school in it. It wanted the school taken off its hands.

Cyril Taylor had warned Kenneth Baker that companies would

not contribute the £8-10 million originally expected. One of Mr Baker's strengths as a politician is said to be his ability to ignore expert advice if it conflicts with what he wants to do.

Almost as worrying was the quality of the sponsors who were coming forward. The household name companies, the respectable companies with respected community relations programmes, were refusing to have anything to do with CTCs. By 1988, the Prime Minister herself was reduced to ringing top company chairmen personally, unsuccessfully trying to persuade them to sponsor CTCs.

British Petroleum (BP) had at that time one of the most extensive and thoughtful community programmes of any company in Britain. In 1988, its sophisticated community affairs department spent £9 – £1.9 million of it on education. But BP defied all efforts to persuade it to sponsor a CTC. BP's then educational adviser Jeremy Nicholls said:

> Companies with a strong tradition of local community support and partnership have tended not to support CTCs. The problem is that companies want to make friends in the communities where they operate. They do not support high profile initiatives which are seen by many people in those communities as divisive.
>
> There was a feeling that CTCs were going to focus a lot of resources on a few children. We want UK plc to invest in the future of all its children.
>
> We were also unhappy about the confusion of an educational agenda with a political agenda. The country needs to find means of educating more people to a higher level. The taxpayer at large is the proper person to pay for these things, rather than the BP shareholder.

So CTC sponsors tended to be smaller companies, headed by the sort of businessman whose admirers call him buccaneering, and whose enemies call him nothing at all unless they have their lawyers present. They often strongly support the Thatcherite wing of the Conservative Party.

Mr Michael Ashcroft is chairman of Bermuda-registered security systems company ADT and a guarantor of the Conservative Party's overdraft. In 1989 Mr Ashcroft tried to set up a CTC in Barnet, north London, but grew impatient with the local council. The Conservative council leader, Roy Shutz, says: 'I think he felt we were a little slow and bureaucratic, wanting to go through committees and consult interested parties.' So Mr Ashcroft took his patronage off to Mrs Thatcher's flagship London borough of Wandsworth.

Wandsworth obliged very quickly. The ADT CTC was a snip to Mr Ashcroft at £1 million. By January 1990 he was able to write to council leader Sir Paul Beresford:

> From a political point of view the higher the profile that can be given to the creation of the CTC concept in Wandsworth the better, and no doubt this will be of much help to your local Conservative candidates for the May 1990 elections.
>
> I have therefore suggested to the Prime Minister and Kenneth Baker that it would be helpful if a small ceremony could be held on or around April 2 1990 so that the college can be formally handed over from the London Residuary Body to the new ADT CTC Trust. The Prime Minister's presence would of course guarantee publicity.

The letter was leaked to Labour education spokesman Jack Straw.

Soon after, Mr Ashcroft's energies were directed elsewhere. He was accused of fraud in the United States, and an investigation into ADT's affairs was triggered by his creditor banks.

Even so, he was considered one of the more suitable CTC sponsors. In 1988 there was a parliamentary row over Kenneth Baker's decision to accept sponsorship from British American Tobacco for a CTC in Middlesbrough. The idea of a tobacco company being able to buy a prominent role in the running of a school, and put its name on the school, helped to discredit the CTC concept.

But even BAT seemed a more suitable sponsor than Brighton property speculator Mr Ivor Revere, whose aborted CTC in Sussex triggered a National Audit Office investigation. Mr Revere suggested to Cyril Taylor's CTC Trust that there should be a CTC on the site of a former Catholic school which the Catholic church was selling. He would provide £1 million and raise £800,000 from other sponsors, and the government would supply £7.2 million.

Mr Revere told the CTC Trust that he intended to offer £2.5 million for the site, though this was less than he thought it was worth. In fact, he persuaded the Catholic Church to accept £2.3 million.

He did not trouble to tell the Church that he wanted it for a CTC. Catholic educationalists have always been critical of CTCs. The church authorities thought he wanted it for a housing development, and were furious when they discovered the truth, believing, like most other people in the area concerned with education, that if the government had £7.2 million to put into Sussex education, there were better ways of using it than sinking it in Mr Revere's school.

Mr Revere transferred the site to the government for £2.5 million. Several months later, it was discovered that he had only paid £2.3 million for it. An embarrassed CTC Trust eventually retrieved the £200,000 difference from Mr Revere's company. Very soon

after that, Mr Revere withdrew his sponsorship, and there is no
Brighton CTC.

The government was left with a disused Sussex school whose
value was declining. It was still unsold four years later, in May
1993. It was costing £1,000 a week for Group 4 Security to look
after it, and Group 4's bill was almost £200,000. It was on the
market for £1.5 million, or £800,000 less than the CTC Trust
bought it for. £1 million has been spent for nothing, and the site
is still unsold.

If civil servants or a local authority had lost £1 million of public money through doing deals with property developers like Mr
Revere, Conservative politicians would be howling with self-righ-
teous rage, and those responsible would probably lose their jobs.

The last CTC to be authorised, in April 1991, was Kingswood,
in Bristol. There was the by now familiar desperate scramble for
sponsors to pay even a small part of the money, to make the thing
look respectable. Eventually, after much arm-twisting, Lord Young,
former Conservative Party chairman and now executive chairman
of Cable and Wireless, came to the rescue. Cable and Wireless and
the Wolfson Trust together put up £2 million, and the government
gratefully coughed up the other £8 million.

Avon County Council's deputy director of education Edward
Watson made a by now familiar point. He said that £8 million of
public money for 900 children at the CTC contrasted starkly with
the £4.5 million which Avon had for capital expenditure on the
county's other 150,000 children.

With that money, he said, all secondary schools in Kingswood
could be fully repaired, all improvements they asked for could be
done, all could have a new science laboratory, and there would be
enough left over to give all primary schools an extra nursery class
for a year.

Kenneth Clarke, who was by now the Education Secretary,
announced the Bristol CTC with a fanfare: '...one of the most
successful features of the government's educational and inner cities
policies...partnership between government and the private sector
...outstanding new colleges...resounding success...welcome the
investment which these important public companies and public-
spirited businessmen are making...'

It was a smokescreen to cover headlong retreat. Business was
not willing to make CTCs work. Instead, Mr Taylor (by now Sir
Cyril in recognition, apparently, of his services to education) was
working on ways of making it cheaper for businesses to sponsor

CTCs, and place a larger share on the public purse.

He came up with them. Unfortunately, they needed changes in the law, and there was a general election due soon. Labour education spokesman Jack Straw was unlikely to oblige. He was horrified by the amount of public money that had already gone into educating a handful of children – more, he pointed out, than the government was spending on the introduction of the national curriculum.

But the Conservatives won, and at the time of writing are preparing to introduce the necessary changes in the law so that Sir Cyril can offer CTCs – to be renamed Technology Colleges – at the bargain basement price of £50,000.

Instead of going to the expense of creating a whole new school, the CTC Trust will simply take over an existing grant maintained school. The governors will hand it over without cost. They will get in return the CTC Trust's expertise in technology and mathematics teaching, and access to a large pot of public money.

The government is expected to say that the sponsor need only provide about £50,000. In return, the sponsor will get four seats on a 16-strong governing body. This requires a change in the law. At the time of writing, there is no legal provision for sponsor governors.

The 'monument principle' is to be abandoned. But, says Sir Cyril, 'there will be a requirement to change the ethic of the school. They cannot just come in for the money.' Technology Colleges must show that they are concentrating on science, mathematics and technology.

Voluntary aided schools and schools controlled by the local education authority will also be able to become Technology Colleges. The government will change the law to allow LEAs to be sponsors. The idea is that the education authority will give – instead of, as before, selling – an existing school to a new foundation run jointly by the LEA, the government and the sponsor.

A word from our sponsor

'Dear parents,' wrote Mrs Pat Elliott, head teacher of Westcliff High School for Girls in Essex, in May 1991. 'We have been aware for some time of the difficulty of obtaining our regulation school skirt. Following discussions with Alexander's of Rayleigh, we have decided to change the style of our skirt, standardise the length of jumper, and allow Alexander's to be our sole supplier. Therefore, only items of uniform purchased from Alexander's will be acceptable.'

The letter did not mention that Alexander's is making substantial contributions to school funds.

Unsurprisingly, Mrs Veronica Emery, of rival school outfitters Klobber, was furious. Five local schools had recently made Alexander's their sole supplier. Mrs Emery's sales had slumped. She felt the schools were trying to put her out of business.

She also resented the implication that she does not understand Westcliff High School's requirements. 'I know exactly what their requirements are. My two daughters went to that school. I have been dressing their girls for years, until this year.

'The school is making money from this, but it is the parents who are paying. Alexander's is more expensive than my shop, and that makes a big difference to the single parents at the school. At my shop, a complete outfit for a 12 or 13 year old girl costs between £90 and £150. The school is making its parents pay about £200.'

Alexander's agree that they are more expensive, but say their clothes are better quality. Mrs Emery hotly denies this. Parents do not have the option of making up their own minds.

In the past, says Mrs Emery, 'it was up to me to provide better quality, price and service to win more customers. Now head teachers are telling parents that they may only purchase from one source, even if another shop can provide the correct style and colour.'

Mrs Elliott gives exact instructions about what the girls must wear, starting with 'navy blue regulation knee-length skirt one style as supplied by Alexanders'. There is a tearoff slip which parents must sign to say they have read the letter, presumably in case an errant parent feigns ignorance of the edict.

Alexander's have undertaken to make sure its assistants understand precisely the school's requirements. This is important to Mrs Elliott, for she does not trust parents not to let their daughters get away with infringements.

'Pupils easily persuade their parents, telling them that all the other girls have short skirts,' says Mrs Elliott. 'When you say navy blue, there is a whole range of navy blues. Pupils always push these things to the limit.

'We were getting,' she adds with distaste, 'to a point where any old navy blue could be Westcliff Girls High School.'

She looks forward to the day when 'all pupils will wear a jersey we have commissioned, with the school logo on it'.

Logo? That is what we used to call the school badge. Schools are forced to see their pupils as the bearers of their corporate identity. Tesco's vans all bear Tesco's logo, so why not Westcliff

High's pupils? We can now look forward to the day when the school song becomes the school jingle, and Saatchi and Saatchi are commissioned to replace the old-fashioned Latin motto with an impactful and up-to-date slogan.

There are two problems for Westcliff High, and for most other British state schools.

The first is that school budgets are being heavily cut, and they are encouraged to look to private companies for finance. Local management of schools means that they have a certain, inadequate, amount from public funds. If they want more than this sum pays for, they must raise it. It is hard to turn down sponsorship money from a clothing firm, even if the price you pay is to give the firm a protected market.

The second also arises directly from government policy. There is now enormous pressure on schools to compete for the pupils thought most likely to succeed. Schools which do not attract the most able pupils will, under the present system, rapidly become labelled as sink schools, and will be reduced to taking the pupils no one else will teach.

Westcliff High is a grammar school, and relies on its local reputation to continue to be over-subscribed. Mrs Elliott puts it this way: 'We wish to create a good image to attract parents. We are keenly aware that we are judged by the appearance of our pupils.'

It is not only clothes shops which sponsor schools. Local companies are sponsoring schools in an increasing number of ways.

Some of them are quite harmless. Companies provide, say, modest prizes for the raffle at the school fête, and are quite content to get in return a mention in the programme.

If they provide things for the school itself, they normally expect a little more. Parents find their children bringing home letters about the services a company offers. The school, if it has any sense, will have extracted a price for using its pupils to carry advertising.

Albany Life Insurance sponsored the renovation of the modern languages room at Allertonshire School in Northallerton, North Yorkshire. Parents at the school received a letter inviting them to a 'financial services seminar' run by Albany Life Assurance. Albany Life has agreed that if it gets customers from the seminar, it will sponsor something else for the school.

It sounds harmless, but there is a difficult principle here. The parents, by giving their money to Albany Life, are buying basic equipment for their children's school. If the parents cannot afford the services of Albany Life, the school goes without.

The system makes a cruel mockery of Britain's boast to provide free education for all.

Parents of children at Manor Park School in Nuneaton, Warwickshire, were offered £10 vouchers for shower units from a local firm, Triton. They were also offered 'starter packs' for their children – school tie, stationery set, sports insurance.

The local education authority put an end to the scheme when it discovered that Triton's managing director was a school governor. But the power of LEAs to put an end to schemes of this nature is rapidly being stripped away as the government provides large sums of money to induce schools to opt out of LEA control.

Kent schools get £95 every two months for putting up advertising posters. Copperfield County Middle School in Milton Keynes gets £1 for every pupil who opens an account at the school branch of Barclays Bank. Barclays has branches in more than 200 schools. The Midland Bank has paid over 1,000 schools £100 each for the right to set up a bank in the school.

These sums are small. Many schools are not yet sophisticated about negotiating these deals. To the school, if someone asks that a letter should be given to every child to take home, this seems a small favour, amply compensated for by, say, a book for the library.

One Barnet primary school handed out letters to take home to parents from a local tennis club, offering lessons for children, to all its five and six year olds. It asked nothing in return for this impeccably targeted advertising – the tennis club even refused to offer a raffle prize.

To a commercial organisation, the chance to target five and six year old children or their parents is worth a great deal. No one other than a school can offer it. In some areas, commercial organisations are able to get valuable marketing for practically nothing, from head teachers who do not know the commercial value of what they are selling.

This is already changing. Cash-starved schools are swiftly learning the price of everything. School governors, when they appoint heads, are checking that they understand the commercial world, and can get the best financial deals for their schools.

This is bad news for those who think that the essential skill of a teacher, the skill which ought to win him or her promotion, is teaching and communicating effectively with children.

Computers for schools

Supermaket giant Tesco has come up with the simplest and most effective method yet devised of using schools to increase sales. It offers to give schools computers – which is the one item most schools need badly and cannot afford.

To get the computers, schools trade in vouchers. You get one voucher for every £25 you spend in Tescos.

A Tesco spokesman claimed they were giving computers away 'for nothing'. In fact, seldom has a company been so careful to ensure that it gets every possible penny in profit.

To get a top-of-the-range computer, you have to present vouchers to the value of £100,000. Tesco's standard profit margin is 7.1 per cent. So it is 'giving' a computer for £7,100.

The company does not give the vouchers on sales of cigarettes and petrol, where profit margins are low. And it banned parents from stationing themselves in Tesco's car parks and encouraging childless shoppers to collect their vouchers anyway and hand them over. The company offered the barely credible reason that the ban was to give all schools an equal chance. Cynics thought the real reason was to avoid parting with more computer equipment than absolutely necessary.

Schools circulated parents telling them to shop in Tescos and collect the vouchers. Thousands of parents must have changed their shopping patterns so as to collect the vouchers. I knew parents who counted the cost of their shopping before getting to the checkout. If it came to a few pounds less than a multiple of £25, they added things.

Some schools, unable to collect enough vouchers to get any worthwhile equipment, sold their vouchers to neighbouring schools. Tescos reacted with hurt indignation: 'These schools were exploiting the scheme when we were offering something for nothing.'

But a clearer idea of who was doing the exploiting came from Sandhurst Infant School in Catford, south London. Parents collected 2,000 vouchers by spending £50,000 at Tescos. In return, they got an eight-year-old model with no disk drive. The computer stayed in storage because the school could not afford £60 for a disk drive.

Apart from the greedy way the scheme is run, is there anything wrong with it in principle? I think there is, because computers these days are not a luxury in a school – they are a necessity.

If schools can only buy basic items by collecting supermarket vouchers, then we have given up any pretence that we offer free state education to everyone. In poor areas, where people cannot afford Tescos prices and cannot afford to measure their shopping in £25 units, schools will go without computers.

Sponsored teaching materials

Companies target schoolchildren by sending teaching materials into schools. Schools, which find it increasingly hard to buy teaching materials, have to be grateful for anything they get for free.

In March 1991 the Sugar Bureau sent out, free and unsolicited, 24,000 copies of a pack called Science and Technology for Seasonal Celebrations to every primary school in Britain. The Sugar Bureau is the trade association for the sugar industry, financed by Tate and Lyle and the British Sugar Corporation. The pack is 75 pages long, glossily and attractively presented, in a useful and practical loose leaf binder.

It is designed, the Sugar Bureau explains to teachers, to 'help you deliver the Science and Design Technology components of Key Stages 1 and 2 of the National Curriculum' and it 'introduces children to sound scientific and design technology practice through extensively trialled activities.' It is aimed at 7-11 year olds.

Action and Information on Sugars (AIS) claims that the Sugar Bureau's information is dangerously selective. AIS is a loose voluntary association of dentists, other dental personnel, health professionals and the odd social scientist.

AIS points out that one section of the Sugar Bureau pack 'looks at "good" sources of sugars, implying that sugars are a necessary part of our diet. However sugar is not an essential component, we can live without it.' It is critical of diagrams showing cross-sections of teeth, which 'ignore the role of sugar in the decay process'.

The Sugar Bureau's pack, says AIS, actively encourages sugar consumption. The information is misleading, and differs from government recommendations.

The Sugar Bureau, which has been providing materials for teachers for over a decade, says that the pack was researched, tried out by teachers, and produced with the help of educational consultants, scientists, nutritionists and dentists. 'We represent the sugar industry and we provide accurate scientific information. Much that has been said about sugar in the past is now known to be inaccurate.'

It calls AIS 'a self-appointed action group which regularly lobbies against the sugar industry' and insists on the accuracy of its pack. It admits the information is not always complete: 'Advanced aspects of nutrition are inappropriate for 7-11 year olds.'

The Sugar Bureau pack is just one of a flood of teaching materials going into classrooms from different food producers. The material varies markedly in presentation. Some are excellent, useful and accurate. Others are pure puffs. A very few commit the cardinal sin of not clearly identifying the commercial interests which sponsor them.

According to Sue Dibb, writing in *The Food Magazine*, 'of the 70 sources of educational material circulated to members of the National Association of Home Economics Teachers, two-thirds are produced by food companies, trade associations and marketing boards. Similarly, two-thirds of the Ministry of Agriculture's list of food and agriculture teaching aids are produced by commercial interests.'

The information contained in these aids, as far as it goes, is generally accurate. Ms Dibb's objection is that it is also selective. 'Kelloggs fails to mention the less desirable nutritional role of added sugar in its *Nutrition Guide*. The Meat and Livestock Commission's leaflet on meat production makes no mention of the antibiotics and growth promoters used in animal rearing. The British Egg Information Service fails to mention the less palatable facts of battery farming.'

Heinz ran a national competition asking pupils to devise a 'nutritious canned ready meal using Heinz baked beans as the main ingredient' – pointing out that it already produced barbecue beans, curried beans, beans with mini sausages, beans and burgerbites, and beans and hot dogs in smoky bacon sauce. Spot the commercial plug.

Smiths suggest collecting their crisp packets, and schools which reach their target get free T-shirts for their football teams. Even McDonalds now produces educational material.

Education sponsorship is big business. Food sponsors aiming to reach home economics teachers have their own organisation, Technology with Home Economics Resources in Education.

This organisation is almost comically secretive. It refused to give me any information about itself, or to send me its regular publication for members and teachers, *Resource News*. Its secretary hung the telephone up when I persisted.

It has 122 members and boasts to them of its 'strong lines of communication with senior home economics educationalists at all levels'. The lead headline in the Autumn 1991 issue of *Resource News* underlines its reason for existence: CONSUMER EDUCATION

– A VIGOROUS ELEMENT OF THE CURRICULUM. The paper lists the resources its members produce, and advertises courses run by companies for home economics teachers.

Producing educational materials has an advantage over advertising. It does not have to be checked by the Advertising Standards Authority to see that it is 'legal, decent, honest and truthful'. Those producing material for schools are not subject to any statutory checks at all. Anyone can mail schools with any material they like.

They may follow guidelines produced by the National Consumer Council, but they are under no obligation to do so. The guidelines are, in any case, so unspecific as to have little effect. They are, in theory, supposed to prevent sponsors of educational material from presenting a sales message to children as though it was objective information.

If teachers want interesting, well-produced, graphic material on limited budgets, they have to make use of the material that comes to them free. Jenny Ridgewell, an educational consultant who writes some of the material, says: 'I recently went into a secondary school where the teacher said she was embarrassed that her wall was full of sponsored material.'

Ms Ridgewell insists that such material 'enriches and enlivens' a classroom – and that, in itself, there is no harm in companies producing and sending out teaching aids.

The national curriculum, she says, makes it harder for companies to send out mere promotional material dressed up as educational material. 'Schools now only want materials if they are relevant and pertinent. The national curriculum means that sponsored materials must help them deliver what they have to deliver.'

She thinks the idea, put forward by some nutritionists such as those involved in AIS, that there should be a statutory body to vet the material going into schools, would just be more bureaucracy. But she accepts that the material cannot be completely unbiased.

And that, at root, is the problem. Children are being taught from materials produced by people who have a vested interest. Frequently the materials are actually prepared by respectable educationalists like Ms Ridgewell, but editorial control rests with the sponsor. The educationalists who go into this work, like Ms Ridgewell, must be prepared to find their editorial judgement overruled by the sponsor.

It would be mistaken, as well as impractical, to stop companies from producing their own educational material and sending it to schools. But we should be ensuring that teachers have a choice.

There should be enough public money in the education system to ensure that teachers can buy objective material. They should not be forced to rely on sponsored educational materials.

Cash and the dreaming spires

After their budgets were first slashed in 1981, universities realised that they faced extinction unless they took their services into the market place and their begging bowls into the streets.

The next decade saw a revolution. Today no British university is complete without its business development unit, its marketing department, its corporate image experts and its alumni fundraising team. All were unheard-of on British campuses before 1979. They are not always, necessarily, an adornment to our seats of learning.

The then Education Secretary, Kenneth Baker, told the Committee of Vice Chancellors and Principals in 1988: 'An essential element is for you to build on your success in raising money from private sources, from business and alumni.'

Sponsorship does not come for nothing, as the Open University acknowledges in the literature it sends out to potential sponsors: 'The University is committed to offering continued support in seeking direct and spin-off benefits for sponsors.' It adds, ominously, that the University 'welcomes collaboration and advice from sponsors in...course preparation' though it 'retains final editorial control of its course materials'.

There is no firm evidence about how far the OU goes in resisting 'advice' from sponsors on preparation of the course material. What we do know is that the will to resist 'advice' at the OU was seriously undermined by a series of papers emanating from Sir Keith Joseph's office when Sir Keith was Education Secretary in the early 1980s.

The papers, all to the effect that the OU's teaching was too left-wing, were understood to be indirect threats that OU funding could suffer if its teaching did not become more politically acceptable.

They were taken most seriously at the OU, whose administration connived in an elaborate cover-up to try to deny to the world that they ever existed. Academics have admitted to feeling pressure to take note of the criticisms in preparation of course material. Sir Keith, according to his then political adviser Stuart Sexton, was satisfied that his initiative had an effect.

The fear of withdrawal of private funding, whether a justified fear or not, is likely to bring about a similar level of self-censorship.

Oxford University is sinking £14 million into its fundraising efforts – the Campaign for Oxford – and aims to raise £220 million in five years. The 1981 and 1986 cuts forced Oxford to cut back its spending by 11 per cent, and to leave 140 academic jobs unfilled.

This makes Oxford very sensitive about its image. It has enemies on both political flanks. The new right thinks it is snobbish, self-indulgent and flabby. The left is still alienated by commem balls and carefully manicured accents (even today, nearly half of Oxford's male undergraduates come from public schools).

Much of the Campaign's effort is concentrated on alumni fundraising – getting former students to give money. But it was sponsorship, rather than donations from alumni, which the government wanted Oxford to seek.

In fact, hard-line Thatcherites berated Oxford for trying to raise money from former students at all. It ought to rely solely on sponsorship, so as to make sure it fitted in with industry's view of what a university should be, according to an unsigned article in the *Economist* expressing the views of the Thatcherite right.

The article, a surprisingly bad-tempered one which appeared at a time when relations between Downing Street and Oxford were particularly poor, told Oxford to stop whingeing and being 'apoplectic about Thatcherism' and start running the place like a business.

'It is only four years,' said the *Economist* crossly, 'since the university voted to deny Mrs Margaret Thatcher an honorary degree, the first Prime Minister to have been at Oxford to have been snubbed like that.'

In 1989, Oxford's Chancellor, Lord Jenkins, noted 'with mild dismay that about three-quarters of my conversations with the Vice Chancellor of Oxford is devoted to this subject (raising money). I like to think that, say, Curzon used to talk to Sir Herbert Warren about less mundane matters.'

The Campaign's early successes included saving two chairs threatened with the axe because of shortage of funds. The Chair of Italian Studies, vacant since 1987, was revived with a £700,000 endowment from Fiat. The Chair of Byzantine and Modern Greek Studies was saved by a group of wealthy Greeks in London.

But only the old, prestige universities can raise private money for that sort of purpose. Outside Oxford and Cambridge, company money normally comes for applied science, computer studies, management and business studies. The university which wants to have a faculty studying Italian Studies or Byzantine and Modern Greek

Studies does so in genteel poverty, and must stave off bankruptcy each day.

The era of sponsored chairs is not kind to subjects whose study does not make anyone rich. The Regius Professor of Semiotic Studies in Eleventh Century Lithuania is being elbowed aside by the Polly Peck Professor of Profits.

Keele University had to change the whole balance of its courses in order to stay alive. Fund-raising consultant Dr Carl James advised the university that it had a poor profile for raising money, with too many arts courses.

Led by a new, dynamic and commercially-minded vice-chancellor, Professor Brian Fender, Keele re-negotiated its industrial contracts to bring in a better return. It got soft loans from banks in return for a foothold on the campus. It built a science park, so that industry could rent space on its campus, with the attraction of being close to its research facilities. And it set up a Research, Development and Business Affairs Department.

The danger to academic freedom of too much reliance on sponsorship became obvious to Newcastle University academics in the mid-1980s, when the Saudi Arabian government withdrew sponsorship of a lectureship in Islamic Studies. It considered Dr Denis MacEoin's specialisation in Islamic mysticism to be heretical, and Dr MacEoin lost his job.

It is a rather serious matter that Newcastle University did not feel it could afford the dignity of telling the Saudi government what it could do with its money.

What would be the university's view if an oil-rich government were to offer generous funding for a chair so long as the university first made a bonfire of all works in its library which were written by Salman Rushdie? Given the principle already set, it is hard to see why it should refuse.

Despite this experience, in 1988 Newcastle accepted a £450,000 endowment to create a William Leech Professor of Applied Christian Theology. Applicants had to have 'clear Christian commitment'.

Later, Newcastle accepted a £15,000 grant from British Nuclear Fuels Ltd for a visiting fellowship in government communications for Mr Bernard Ingham, the controversial press secretary to the then Prime Minister, Margaret Thatcher. Newcastle's academics suspected, understandably, that BNFL's motives were not entirely pure. Suspicions were fuelled by the University's admission that if Mr Ingham had not been available, 'it would not have happened'.

Birmingham University has at least five substantially privately

funded chairs, and its public affairs director Frank Albrighton told
the *Observer* in 1990: 'Companies are looking at what return, directly or indirectly, they can get. They are interested in partnership,
seeing research done in a particular field and seeing the output of
high-level graduates maintained. It's imaginative investment rather
than private patronage.'

Reliance on sponsorship is increasing rapidly. In the academic
year 1982-83, Britain had 233 university professorships which were
not wholly financed from the public purse. In the academic year
1987-88 this figure had increased to 382.

The dangers of this trend are increased by the government's
policy of getting rid of pay scales, and paying lecturers whatever
the market will stand. This means that those lectureships able to
attract sponsorship would, and sometimes already do, attract a
considerably higher salary than others.

Jean Bocock of the National Association of Teachers in Further
and Higher Education says: 'The real problem is a shortage of
money in the system to reward people at all levels. Realistic pay
levels are needed for the people who manage the training of social
workers as much as they are needed for the people who manage
the training of accountants.'

The problem for the universities is not the existence of sponsorship. There is little objection to sponsorship, so long as institutions are free to accept or reject it; to look at the small print and
decide whether the price is too high.

The problem arises when public funding is so far reduced that
no sponsorship can be refused, however degrading the conditions,
if it yields a satisfactory profit.

If – to take the Newcastle example – the Saudi government wants
to sponsor Islamic Studies, but wants the right to insist that certain
avenues are not explored, an academic institution with any self-
respect, or any respect for the integrity of its staff, will tell them
to take their money somewhere else.

If a university sets out with a mission to cater especially for arts
and social science students, it should not have to drop all that in
order to turn out a constant supply of Masters of Business Administration specialising in the grummet industry because it has the
misfortune to be situated next door to a grummet company.

In his letter to Oxford graduates in April 1989 launching the
Campaign for Oxford, the then Vice Chancellor, Sir Patrick Neill,
wrote: 'It is my belief that funds from private sources can be used
to great effect to...preserve that independence and freedom of

manoeuvre which is essential to the life of a vigorous academic institution.'

But they can only be so used if you are in a position to turn them down. British universities are approaching the twenty first century 1990s in no such position.

There is another, more practical, reason for ensuring that universities are not desperate for private money. Private money is very expensive to raise. Dr Henry Drucker, the American fund-raiser who is in charge of the Campaign for Oxford, has a staff of about 100, and reckons, on the basis of the American experience, that you have to spend about 10 per cent of the money you hope to get. Oxford University has invested £14 million in the Campaign for Oxford.

You could pay for a lot of university professorships with £14 million.

Compacts and TECs

Although industry has resisted government attempts to make it responsible for Britain's education system, there are some forms of education sponsorship which it is keen on. It likes the sort of scheme which produces tangible results from small investments, together with benefits for the company as well as the community.

Compacts are a good example. A compact is a means of bringing business and schools together. Businesses help and advise schools, providing work experience for pupils and secondment for teachers, as well as help with finding jobs. Schools undertake to listen to companies' advice about the sort of skills they ought to be teaching. Pupils undertake to fulfil the compact goals, which are related to attendance, punctuality and completion of courses.

Businesses which sponsor compacts are required to put into the compact scheme enough seconded managers to run the administration and to spend some time in schools; to provide some places for pupils to go on work experience; and to provide some places for teachers on secondment. They also guarantee to offer a job interview to all the pupils in the compact schools who complete compact goals.

In return, schools guarantee to prepare pupils for the world of work, under the tutelage of the company's secondees.

Compacts were billed as industry contributing to inner city regeneration. Industry is, at the same time, of course, getting a preview of those who will soon be on offer to it as employees. It does not guarantee jobs (though an over-enthusiastic government at first claimed that it did) – only job interviews.

In return for this guarantee, the sponsoring companies get a preview of those who are coming up to school leaving age, and can select those whom they would like to recruit. They do not have to find jobs for any more people than they would have found anyway. Compacts have no effect on unemployment.

Clearly, compact companies stand to gain at least as much as they spend on compacts – probably rather more. Industry likes Compacts.

But it started to like them less when the government seized on the Compact idea as a way of handing yet more of the education system to the private sector. Richard Martineau, the industrialist who brought the Compact concept from Boston to London, was thoroughly alarmed.

'We brought from Boston an idea about partnership. It was dressed up, for political purposes, as a guarantee of a job. This was a sort of Indian rope trick. In the 1991 Education White Paper, the government said it wants to extend the Compact concept to every school in the country. In a recession, this loses credibility.' In 1993, this goal looks as far away as ever.

In fact, more people leave school without a job every year. To get a job, they may need training. In August 1991 the government abolished the old Training Agency, which used to supply it. In future, said ministers, the private sector will provide training. And the private sector has once again proved reluctant.

The national network of 82 Training and Enterprise Councils – TECs – was completed the same year, with £2.4 billion of public money for the financial year 1991-92. TECs were told to plan and run all training and vocational education. Each TEC is a consortium of local businessmen, self-selecting and self-perpetuating.

But businesses, while willing to donate the time of their top people to run the TECs, were not willing to give them much money.

Funding became a battle between industry and the government. Both sides knew that there was not enough money to fulfil the TEC brief, which was to provide a youth training place for every 16-18 year old not in full-time education.

Both sides expected the other to make up the shortfall. So far, neither side has done so, and neither side looks like doing so.

The result is that TECs spend public money – and are accountable to nobody for the way in which they spend it. They are private companies, and even Parliament cannot demand to know what is going on.

Some TECs take the view that they are there to show the flabby public sector how things ought to be done. The Central London TEC – CENTEC – is one of these. I sat in on one of its directors' meetings in 1991. Its chairman, Lord Stockton of Macmillan Publishers Ltd (Harold Macmillan's grandson) told his colleagues: 'We're here to get the business ethos into the education system.'

Everyone nodded. No one was in any doubt that what British education needs is a good dose of business ethos. The chief executive, Gwynneth Flower, wanted secondments in industry for all her top staff to 'show them what goes on in the real world'. More nods. Everyone there knew what the real world is. It is what goes on in the offices of big companies. Everything else is illusion.

Mrs Flower, former sales and marketting manager for GEC Marconi, told me she wanted to teach her 65 staff 'a different culture, a different language'. Lord Stockton explained: 'Our language is the language of the bottom line, of takeovers and banks.'

And that, said Mrs Flower, gesturing magnificently round her own massive office, was why CENTEC had its headquarters in an elegant house in Grosvenor Square and not in 'a dingy grey government building.' The plush private sector trappings were everywhere – but they are purchased with £16 million a year of public money.

Business votes with its feet

After two decades of substantial public funding, education in the eighties was suddenly forced to depend on the whims of business. Business has shown clearly that it intends to button up its purse.

Too many demands are being made on it. Fund-raising consultant Redmond Mullin says that the same people are being hit for money all the time. Charities, with which education must compete, are increasingly being expected to fund services, especially in health, which used to be publicly funded. Universities are poaching fund-raisers and pushing up their salary levels, so that good fund-raisers can cost more than small charities can afford.

The UK has 160,000 charities and 4,000 new ones spring up each year. Some of them are thoroughly unhappy about the activities of education fundraisers. At the same time, many city bosses are saying privately – and occasionally publicly – that they are being asked to pay for too many things which the state ought to be paying for.

Companies are getting more sophisticated about giving, and sponsoring education is not what they like doing best. They do not want

to take over the education system. That, in effect, is what they
were being asked to do when they were invited to sponsor City
Technology Colleges – and we can thank business people for the
failure of that especially absurd and divisive idea.

The companies which are sophisticated about their sponsorship,
and do it on any sort of scale, employ community affairs managers
to keep their work within the company's policies. They like to set
up and monitor schemes themselves. And they like – as Robin
Heal, former Community Affairs Manager at BP, puts it – to do a
lot of good with as little money as possible. If they put money into
the community, they want to see the money hard at work, providing tangible benefits for the company as well as the community.

Britain has a per cent club, modelled on the USA. Member
companies pledge themselves to spending at least half of one per
cent of pre-tax profits on community affairs. It was initiated by
Joel Joffe, deputy chairman of Allied Dunbar, who envisaged companies spending a full one per cent, as many US companies do.
But he met strong resistance to this, and had to settle for half of
one per cent.

British corporate giving is still nowhere near the scale of the USA,
which has a one per cent club, a five per cent club and even a (very
small) 10 per cent club.

'May we,' asked Lord Jenkins, Oxford University's Chancellor, in
the sixth Arnold Goodman lecture in June 1989, 'be left uneasily
poised, in this respect as in some others, between the US and
continental Europe, without the private generosity of the former
or the more adequate public funding of the latter?'

All the signs are that we are in exactly the situation Lord Jenkins
described. The Charities Aid Foundation reckons that corporate
giving averaged 0.61 per cent of pre-tax profits in 1990-91. This
was a slight drop on the previous year. But, because profits were
lower in 1990-91, considerably less money was produced.

In real terms, says CAF, company support for community affairs
is falling. Companies' support for charities, for example, fell by
three per cent in real terms in 1990-91.

So we are not moving towards US levels of corporate support
for the community. We are moving away from them. The gap is
getting bigger.

At the same time, corporate generosity has ever-increasing demands made on it, as the government rolls back the frontiers of the
state and insists that more and more public services should be
funded by corporate generosity rather than through the tax system.

Something has to suffer. Education is bound to be among the first sacrifices. It received the highest level of support from companies in 1990-91. Yet the BP view is gaining ground rapidly in company community affairs departments. Increasingly, business does not consider it ought to be running Britain's education system.

The government strategy was to reduce taxation on big business, and ask business to respond by voluntarily paying for education. This, said ministers, would enable them to serve the purposes of business.

The strategy – oddly for an avowedly pro-business government – showed a fundamental misunderstanding of British business people. Unlike their American counterparts, most of them do not see the running of the education system as the proper role for business. The biggest companies – the household name companies – believe that education should be paid for by the taxpayer in general, not by their shareholders.

But the strategy is much worse than simply impractical. It is also immoral. Schools exist mainly for the benefit of the child, only secondarily for the benefit of the child's future employer, and not at all for those who want to sell the child things.

Britain's education system will not begin its recovery until we have a government which understands this simple and obvious truth.

MICHAEL O'CONNOR & MICHAEL RAYNER

Sponsorship and Health

Introduction

Health would seem to be an obvious choice for a company deciding how to spend its sponsorship money.

There can be few areas more likely to produce the warm glow that sponsors seek to generate in the public's heart. The benefits of the "glow" may be indirect for sponsors with no immediate commercial interest in health, but the benefits are more direct, and probably more lucrative, for those with commercial interests in health care.

Interest in health sponsorship is growing according to a report from the market research agency Mintel. An increasing number of businesses from all sectors are becoming aware of the benefits of sponsorship in social and educational areas. Mintel expects such sponsorship to grow significantly in the next decade. It sees companies wanting to project a responsible image which will be of increasing importance in the 'caring sharing' 1990s. Even if these sentiments melt away in an increasingly competitive world market, it looks as if sponsorship of health will continue to make good economic sense.

One reason why such sponsorship is growing is rooted in wider economic and social changes. As people become more affluent they spend a growing proportion of their income on health related products.

The health care market is now very large, accounting for over six per cent of the UK's Gross Domestic Product. The private sector, the main source of sponsorship, is taking a growing share of the health care market and the present Government shows signs of wanting to see that share increasing.

Access to the health care market for commercial suppliers has improved with the growth of private medical care. But if the market has grown, it has also become more competitive. Consumers have become more and more cynical over the last twenty years. They are increasingly sceptical about what they are told in traditional advertising. In the US the actions of campaigners such as Ralph Nader and Sidney Wolfe in exposing unethical practices in marketing products ranging from cigarettes to body scanners have contributed towards this trend. In the UK successive governments have seen the need for semi-autonomous agencies, such as the

National Consumer Council to protect the interests of consumers. The phenomenal growth in circulation of the Consumers' Association magazine *Which?* is one sign of the growing demand from consumers for independent information about the goods and services they are being encouraged to buy. At a more fundamental level the threat posed to the environment by the consumer society has made people question the ethics of consumption upon which many companies depend.

Faced with these trends many large organisations realise that they need to find new ways of promoting their products and to be seen as "responsible". Some companies have put efforts into the direct rehabilitation of their image, e.g. oil pipelines which do not disrupt the landscape. However for many this is an expensive option. Far cheaper is the strategy of becoming associated with something people approve of and value, such as the arts or health.

Yet it seems that commercial sponsors have not been entirely successful in eliminating public cynicism about their motives. The Mintel survey found that consumers have a clear understanding of the role of sponsorship. They realise that sponsorship is arranged on commercial grounds rather than purely altruistic ones. Most consider that companies sponsor because it is simply a form of advertising or because it creates a good image for the company. Consumers also have firm opinions as to what is and what is not acceptable sponsorship. Only four out of ten believe that sponsorship of health care is acceptable. Despite this reported cynicism sponsors clearly still believe that sponsorship represents good value for money.

Where the sponsorship money is being spent

Sponsorship in health is currently concentrated in two areas: research and education. There is a small amount spent on actual medical services.

Most people working in the health field consider that research – both basic and applied – is fundamental to their work. Improvements in public health flow from the discovery of knowledge and techniques, allied to the social will to make these findings available to people in a form that they can use. How the fruits of research are made available to people is the subject of continuing argument but it is generally agreed there is a continuing need to produce more "fruit".

The other area which is of central importance is the education of health professionals and the public. Health professionals have to be trained in the basics of medicine – i.e. the findings of medical research – before they are allowed to practice. In recent years there has been a growing belief that the more people know about their own health the more they can take control of it. To an extent this is agreed by both left and right on the political spectrum. The Left seeks to democratise health by shifting power from a male dominated medical élite to communities, while the Right wants to shift some of the responsibility for health care from the State to the individual.

Therefore a consensus has developed on the importance of educating the public about their health and of making them more responsible for it. They are being exhorted to adopt a more healthy lifestyle by changing what they eat, quitting smoking, limiting alcohol intake and taking more exercise. Commercial sponsors are interested in these trends where they have implications for their sales – not just of existing products but, in many cases, new products which are introduced to take advantage of these trends.

Finally the direct sponsorship of medical care might seem to be an attractive option. Until the establishment of the National Health Service a significant proportion of medical care was funded from charitable sources, some of which were associated with commercial agencies. However the actual provision of medical services is now rarely sponsored as most of the funding comes from the Government. Sponsoring routine medical care would be a prohibitively expensive option. More likely is the sponsorship of hospital buildings or of innovative forms of care in order to gain kudos from involvement in new forms of treatment.

Research

Medical research is very expensive. It consumes vast sums in financial and human terms. It is said, for example, that in any one year more people are employed in the UK to find a cure for cancer than die from the disease.

Experience in medical research is now almost a prerequisite for professional advancement for doctors. In a survey of its members carried out by the Royal College of Physicians 85% of doctors said that they had attempted some form of research and 80% considered that research experience would be highly regarded by consultant appointment committees. A total of 60% thought research necessary for career advancement. Research is increasingly necessary for other ambitious health professionals – nurses, pharmacists, dietitians and others.

Not only is more and more research undertaken, but that research has become increasingly expensive. Prior to this century, most medical research was carried out by doctors as a sideline to their medical practice and was mainly observational in nature. With the development of experimental approaches to medical research in this century funding from government, charitable or commercial sources has become ever more necessary to cover the cost of purpose-built laboratories, increasingly complex equipment, growing numbers of staff.

Commercial sponsorship of medical research has a long history involving many well known industrialists. Lord Nuffield (who made his fortune from Morris cars), the Rockefeller family (banking) Henry Wellcome (drugs), all spent large amounts of their accumulated wealth in setting up charitable trusts from which to fund medical research. Some of the current funding for medical research still comes from these trusts and foundations – the Wellcome Trust, for example, now spends £64 million a year on medical research.

Much of the current funding for medical research comes directly from commercial agencies, particularly the pharmaceutical industry, although the food industry is increasingly becoming involved, with the growing recognition of the relationship between food and health. Another sector with a growing interest in medical research is the insurance industry.

Part of the pharmaceutical industry money is spent on in-house research, but some estimates indicate that at least 60% is spent through universities and hospitals. However it is spent the expenditure is huge. In 1990/91 the pharmaceutical industry spent £1,082 million compared with £186 million by the government and £192 million by medical research charities.

Commercial sponsorship of research takes various forms. Companies sometimes provide core funding for research institutions, for example by funding new buildings or equipment. Thirty-one drug companies are named as benefactors on the commemorative plaque on the building at the Hammersmith Hospital that houses the Department of Clinical Pharmacology. Sometimes completely new institutes are created within an older academic setting, for example the Sandoz Institute in University College London. Sometimes existing departments are bought up as Squibb has done with the Department of Pharmacology at Oxford University for £21 million.

More commonly the funding takes the form of grants for specific research projects. Pharmaceutical companies are mainly concerned to fund research related to the development of drugs – particularly trials of new drugs – but they also commit resources to areas as diverse as general practice management and attitudes to and beliefs about health amongst the public. The food industry principally funds nutrition research. The insurance industry is interested in issues related to life expectancy. For example Allied Dunbar have recently funded an important survey of levels of fitness in the UK in partnership with the Health Education Authority.

A particular case of commercial sponsorship of research merits special mention. For some years there has been growing pressure for a ban on tobacco advertising. After an initial legislative phase when tobacco advertising on television was banned, governments of both main political persuasions have resisted a total ban and relied instead on unenforceable agreements (sometimes called 'voluntary') with the tobacco industry which regulate what advertisements show and where they are placed. These measures do not seriously restrict the industry's ability to promote their product. However a ban on television advertising in 1965 was painful for the industry and so this was undermined by massive sponsorship of televised sporting events. This was so successful that recent surveys show that most children believe tobacco is in fact advertised on television. But the tobacco industry also attempted to use the public relations advantages of sponsorship of medical research. When in 1982 the Government announced a new voluntary agreement the then Secretary of State for Social Services, Norman Fowler, announced the setting up of the Health Promotion Research Trust. It was funded by a grant of £11 million from the tobacco industry and its terms of reference were to promote health by 'commissioning, funding and making appropriate provision for the dissemination of the results of a balanced programme of research (other than studies designed directly or indirectly to examine the use and effects of tobacco products)...'

This last exclusion caused a storm of protest. The British Medical Association called the exclusion disgraceful and urged doctors not to cooperate with people who accepted money from the Trust. The Health Education Council withheld grants from academics who accepted money from the Trust. The establishment of the Trust was widely seen as an attempt by the tobacco industry to present itself in a favourable light and to divert attention from tobacco as a cause of ill health. In the words of one medical commentator it was like 'the Mafia funding research into the promotion of law and order but ruling out the topic of organised crime'. The government did itself no credit by being seen to be in collusion with the tobacco industry.

The tobacco industry has a long history of sponsoring health research. While the Health Promotion Research Trust was a clear case of diversionary tactics the industry has gone so far as to try to undermine the basic research into the link between smoking and lung cancer. In the early 1950s, when the early work of Doll and Hill was showing clear evidence of a link between cancer and smoking, the tobacco industry tried to undermine their work. They were unsuccessful in this endeavour as the strength of the evidence grew, but the Government were remarkably slow to back Doll and Hill's work. When, in 1954, they moved towards making a public statement UK tobacco companies offered the Medical Research Council the then princely sum of £250,000 for further research into the subject. The Government were clearly aware of the sensitivity of accepting such money and the decision to accept it was finally taken by full Cabinet in February 1954. The donation was timed to coincide with the Government's public statement and so the industry had their donation announcement at the same time as the Government made its announcement on the health implications of smoking: an excellent example of public relations damage limitation.

In any sponsorship arrangement it is important to the sponsor to promote the image of partnership with the recipient. Once again the tobacco industry managed to do this with the donation of more than £1 million to the Tobacco Products Research Trust. This Trust, managed by the Independent Scientific Committee on Smoking and Health, a Government appointed body, was set up to look at the way the reduction of tar yield from cigarettes led to less serious health consequences. Throughout developed economies the tobacco industry has been reducing tar yield as a way of promoting the concept of 'safe cigarettes' in the face of the growth in public awareness that smoking kills. Through this sponsorship the tobacco industry bought a partnership with government in promoting the, largely irrelevant, concept of safer cigarettes.

Does the sponsor influence research?

The source of funding for medical research inevitably influences the type of medical research that is undertaken. All funding agencies have some sort of policy on the type of research they fund. For example the Wellcome Trust does not fund research into cancer taking the view that sufficient funding for research in this area is available from elsewhere. However the nature of the commercial interests of some large funders has more worrying implications for research and the resulting knowledge base. In the final analysis the aim of the largest funders, the pharmaceutical industry, is to sell drugs. Consequently medical knowledge relating to drug treatment is much more extensive than that underpinning preventive measures. The structure of the knowledge base reflects the need to secure ends suiting the commercial objectives of the major commercial sponsors. There are few signs that the Government and independent charities see it as their responsibility to redress this imbalance.

Commercial sponsorship may not only influence the type of medical research carried out but it may also affect the outcome of that research. An industry perspective on whether sponsorship of research by industry influences outcome was given at the Twelfth Annual Meeting of the World Sugar Research Organisation in a paper entitled *The life cycle of funding committees and the basis of committee decisions* by Professor John Reid, Deputy Principal of the University of Cape Town. The contents of this paper are described in detail in *The Politics of Food* by Geoffrey Cannon (Century, 1987).

Reid explained how commercial concerns – in this case the sugar industry – should fund scientists in order to 'improve and communicate scientific information'. In particular he addressed the issue of 'what produces maximum benefit' to the sponsoring body in relation to the cost; for example whether it is best to support a promising scientist or a promising research proposal.

> If you have located a person whom you have confidence in as a research worker and as one who will keep your needs in mind and not just use your money – then to go on supporting him is much cheaper than assembling panels of experts to vet in great detail the research proposal, engaging in negotiation to alter here and improve there.

How precise should be the requirements of the funding organisation when seeking to influence the type of research which relates to the interests of the funding body? Professor Reid recommends casting a wide net:

Let us take the case of dental caries. Should one say to the research fraternity at large – caries is the problem, let's hear from you? Or immunisation against caries is the name of the game: let's have the proposals? I am a believer in one side of this: the side that does not specify but leaves it open. That way you actually enlist the services of the whole research fraternity in determining where the likely pay off projects are to be located. You can apply your own criteria at a later stage of the process of deciding who and what to support.

Can a sponsor actually influence the outcome of the research they fund? Professor Reid again:

There is a hidden agenda in the research support business. Those who accept your support are often perceived to be less likely to give you a bad scientific press. They may come up with the results that cause you problems, but they will put them in a context in a way that leaves you happier than had they emanated from someone not receiving your support. My own observation and comment is that this hidden effect is powerful – more powerful certainly than we care to state loudly, either from the point of view of the honour in science or in industry. It takes a lot to bite the hand that feeds you: a muzzle is a good insurance against unwelcome bites.

Discussion

It would seem to be uncontentious that a free market in research funding will have implications for the nature of the knowledge base. Big money will fund big research. If there are few commercial spin-offs it is unlikely that sponsorship will be easy to come by. Should society be concerned about this? Not if the market economy is so structured that all humankind's needs are reflected in commercial activities. If everything we need can be bought and sold then, it is argued, it will pay someone to research better products to meet our needs. Those products most prized, or whose production or further refinement is most avidly sought, will be the most profitable and will attract large research budgets. This clearly works in some circumstances. The discovery of a vaccine against the Human Immunodefficiency Virus (HIV) would be both a boon to humankind and a highly profitable product for the discoverer. Pharmaceutical companies are rightly spending vast amounts on research into identifying a vaccine. However for this model to work fully there must be a faultless articulation between human needs and economic power. This is not the case. This simplistic model also supposes a clockwork world undisturbed by the perturbations of human folly. One only has to look at the amount of research devoted to finding more efficient means of killing one another to realise how foolish we can be. If there is concern about commercial sponsorship of medical research, is there anything that can be done about it in a free market economy? It is hard to believe that banning sponsorship of research will ever be seen as desirable or even possible. However in order to maintain research into less commercially attractive subjects it is important that Government and independent charities maintain their commitment to research.

It is less clear whether the source of sponsorship influences the actual outcome of research. There is a perception that this is the case. For example people many who believe the UK population consume too much saturated fat for their good health look askance at research in this area funded by butter manufacturers. Many researchers however would throw up their hands in horror at the suggestion that they "doctored" their results in any way. If the source of funding does have any influence it is likely to be in much more subtle ways than falsification of results. The choice of experimental design, the decision of which experimental results to highlight, the importance laid on 'bad' results are all sources of potential bias which the researcher can introduce in the interest of pleasing the sponsor and perhaps gaining a further contract. Not all of these activities would be visible to peer review – the traditional guardian of sound research. Of course these practices could also occur with publicly funded research and where the state is the only funder the position may be even worse.

The way results are published is another way in which a sponsor can have an influence. Facts rarely speak for themselves: they speak loudest when they are broadcast most widely. Doctors are constantly bombarded with the results of research sponsored by drug companies. When commercial sponsors are not interested in the results of the research they have sponsored then those results are less widely publicised.

In some cases the sponsor may control whether the results are published at all. It is clearly in the sponsors' interests not to publish results which are obviously unfavourable. Such suppression is not the preserve of commercial sponsors. Current government research contracts reserve the right to allow publication and in the past researchers were also subject to the draconian strictures of the Official Secrets Act. However, while all sponsors have power over research results, publicly funded authorities may be more easily accountable for their actions.

It will never be possible to stop researchers wanting to please their sponsors and it is probably impractical to try and guarantee publication rights to some independent agency, as some have suggested. However, government could ensure that the principle of freedom of information extends to commercial disclosure of any research results which have a bearing on the safety or efficacy of consumer products. The research community also has a responsibility to ensure high standards of conduct. Collective organisations representing researchers have an useful role to play to this end.

Education

Sponsors are interested in the education of two audiences: health professionals and the public. Pharmaceutical companies have long been involved in medical education primarily because they want to influence those who take the decisions on drug buying. With the growing emphasis on prevention rather than cure in many areas of medicine, commercial sponsors are increasingly interested in educating the public about health matters, particularly on issues related to their commercial interests.

EDUCATION OF HEALTH PROFESSIONALS:

Colleges
The Royal Colleges, which have an important role in the education of health professionals, have frequently turned to commercial sponsors – particularly the pharmaceutical industry – for support for their journals or projects. A priming fund of £105,000 from Glaxo, Wellcome and Beecham was central to the establishment of the Royal College of General Practitioners in the early 1950s. Green College in Oxford for postgraduate medical students was established with a grant from Cecil Green who had made his money by establishing Texas Instruments. The highly prestigious London School of Hygiene and Topical Medicine was set up with help from the Rockefeller Foundation.

Courses
There has been a considerable development of postgraduate medical centres and of graduate medical education in the last 25 years. Under the terms of their contract, General Practitioners have to attend a minimum number of training courses every year to qualify for a Post Graduate Education Allowance. Possibly because the Department of Health has been slow in giving adequate support to the running of training courses, drug companies have begun to sponsor educational meetings and in some postgraduate medical centres almost every meeting is dependent upon funding from a

pharmaceutical company. The National Association of Clinical Tutors has expressed concern that there is not always appropriate separation of promotional and education activities. The Royal College of Physicians, in commenting on the practice of drug company sponsorship, noted that 'It is convenient for many of these meetings to take place at lunchtime or in the evening and it is reasonable that light refreshments should be available. We regret that this refreshment is so often sponsored by pharmaceutical companies. As a regular practice this degrades our profession.'

Some commercial companies will pay for individuals to travel to foreign countries to study health issues. This type of sponsorship ranges from manufacturers of garlic capsules paying for people to visit foreign manufacturing sites, to companies such as Van den Berghs, who manufacture Flora margarine, holding study trips for health journalists. It would seem likely that one of the aims of these trips is to inculcate a favourable view of the sponsor's goods.

Conferences

Hardly a medical conference is now held which is not to some extent sponsored by commercial interests. The sponsors are normally pharmaceutical companies but in the area of preventive health care the food industry is increasingly interested in providing sponsorship.

Typically pharmaceutical companies will pay most of the costs of running the conference. Some delegates may be required to pay a registration fee but the sponsors will subsidise the accommodation, the food, the conference report, etc. Most of the programme content will normally be decided by an independent medical body – often a Royal College or some other prestigious medical organisation – but special sessions will be organised by the sponsors. The expenses of the organising committee, the speakers and the session chairs are likely to be paid in full and they may also be paid a handsome honorarium. Funding will often be provided for some individuals to attend these conferences. Upon arrival delegates will find that the conference hall is dwarfed by the display of sponsors' products, from high technology equipment to booths offering hospitality mixed with glossy brochures extolling the virtues of certain drugs.

The cost of these conferences can be enormous. To take one example, the week-long European Society of Cardiology conference in Nice in 1989 was attended by over 11,000 people. It is by no means the biggest conference on the annual schedule of cardiology conferences but at a conservative estimate the full economic cost of each person's attendance must have been at least £1,000 when account is taken of travel, accommodation, registration and opportunity costs. This means that the cost of the conference exceeded the amount spent in that year by the UK Government in preventing coronary heart disease.

A proposed European Community directive covering the promotion of drugs could curtail the sponsorship of conferences by the pharmaceutical industry. Needless to say this is being vigorously opposed by the industry. The Pharmaceutical Price Regulation Scheme, under which the price paid by the NHS for drugs is regulated, currently allows up to nine per cent of the price of a drug to be spent on promotion.

Educating the public

Mortality and morbidity rates from the most common fatal diseases in the United Kingdom – coronary heart disease and cancer – remain persistently high despite recent advances in their treatment. Moreover newly emerging diseases such as AIDS are still incurable. Therefore prevention rather than cure is increasingly regarded as the most effective way of improving the health of the public. In most cases prevention chiefly consists of urging people to change their lifestyle by means of health education about the dangers of unhealthy lifestyles.

There are many reasons why commercial sponsors should wish to become involved with health education. In particular the food industry is concerned to improve its image in the face of a widespread concerns about food safety and increasing recognition that the UK diet is too high in fat, particularly saturated fat, sugar and salt, and too low in fibre, starch, and certain vitamins and minerals. Quite naturally companies wish to promote their own products in an environment where many people are being urged to change their diet in the interests of health.

The prevention of disease by means of lifestyle change is a challenge for pharmaceutical companies: if less people become ill there may be less demand for drugs. However, the new climate also creates new opportunities for the industry. For example, if people fail to give up smoking on their own they may be prescribed drugs – nicotine chewing gum, nicotine patches – to help them; if blood cholesterol levels fail to fall when a person tries to change their diet then they may be prescribed lipid lowering drugs.

There is also increasing emphasis on the need to educate the public about the benefits of drugs. For example a new directive from the European Community will require pharmaceutical companies to produce literature to accompany drugs giving details of how and when to take them, their side effects, methods of storage, etc.

The pharmaceutical industry has supported this directive because it believes that provision of better patient information will help to improve its image. However this desire for openness does not extend to all information about drugs. The pharmaceutical industry has recently opposed a Private Member's Bill introduced by Giles Radice MP which aimed to make it possible for the results of drug trials to be disclosed to the public.

The law does not allow the pharmaceutical industry to promote prescription drugs directly to the public: they can only target medical personnel through trade magazines etc. In many cases it is unlikely that pharmaceutical companies would ever wish to advertise direct to the public as the details of individual drugs are often highly complex. Yet in some cases they would find it advantageous. For example, influenza vaccination uptake in the UK is low compared to the US and some European countries. Vaccination is voluntary and it would clearly benefit the manufacturers to encourage people to come forward. Yet the industry cannot openly solicit customers.

One way of circumventing the restrictions is for pharmaceutical companies to sponsor charities amongst whose clientele they would expect to draw customers, e.g. charities for the elderly, for people with specific diseases, etc. For example SANE, a charity caring for people suffering from schizophrenia, lists the pharmaceutical companies Sandoz and Lundbeck as supporters among a range of others from Guinness to National Power. Many charities see this as fairly innocuous but the experience of the Terrence Higgins Trust highlights some of the potential pitfalls. Wellcome manufactures AZT, a drug used in the treatment of AIDS. Wellcome provided financial support to the Terrence Higgins Trust which is a charity set up to promote the interests of people who are HIV positive or suffer from AIDS. In 1993 early results of a new trial of AZT suggested that the drug was not as beneficial as had been hoped in the treatment of people who were HIV positive but who had not yet developed AIDS. The Trust came under heavy criticism from other organisations concerned with AIDS for accepting sponsorship from Wellcome.

Educating the public about health has traditionally involved leaflets, books and posters. Nowadays videos and computer software are also used. These heath education materials are distributed to the public primarily via health professionals and teachers. The few surveys which have been carried out to investigate the sources of health education materials suggest that over half come from a commercial source. The rest are issued by charities or government agencies, but even these materials are frequently sponsored by commercial concerns.

Inaccurate information in health education materials could have serious consequences for health if it leads to the adoption of lifestyles which impair rather than improve health. The source of health education materials can affect their accuracy, balance and other aspects of their content. A recent educational pack for primary schools produced by the Sugar Bureau claims to provide an understanding of the 'meaning and importance of a balanced diet'. However, the information it contains has been seen as misleading by some nutritionists and its recommendations differ from those of recent Government reports. The pack does go into the issue of tooth decay but implies that either starch or sugar can cause cavities whereas starch is 'very much less important than dietary sugars' according to the Health Education Authority.

It is relatively easy to find examples of blatant inaccuracy but since there is little research into the content of health education leaflets it is difficult to know whether they constitute the exception or the rule. What is clear is that many of the commercially produced materials, if not factually incorrect, frequently over-emphasise or underplay particular aspects of current nutritional thinking. Leaflets on healthy eating produced by breakfast cereal manufacturers, for example, over-emphasise the importance of dietary fibre in the diet, and those produced by margarine manufacturers do the same for polyunsaturated fat. Leaflets on diet produced by drug companies are more concerned with the benefits of lipid lowering dugs than healthy eating. Leaflets produced by food manufacturers about the feeding of babies often promote the use of formula foods and milks instead of breast feeding.

Furthermore, commercially sponsored health education materials often blatantly promote the product of the publisher of the materials. A leaflet from the Meat and Livestock Commission purporting to give the consumer dietary advice about blood cholesterol devotes more than half its pages to the nutritional benefits of meat. A survey of commercially sponsored educational materials sent to schools carried out by the National Consumer Council found that over half were promotional rather than educational.

The source of the material affects not only its content but also its credibility. Surveys of attitudes to the source of information about health suggest that the public trust non-commercial more than commercial sources. So commercially funded leaflets are likely to be trusted more when backed or published by a non-commercial agency such as a charity or government body. It is therefore in the interests of commercial producers to gain the endorsement of such bodies for the health related information they put out. The Health Education Authority's *Look After Your Heart* programme has allowed food retailers and trade organisations to use their heart shaped logo on certain leaflets. Some health charities also publish literature funded by food manufacturers and pharmaceutical companies.

Discussion

Sponsorship of activities connected with the education of health professionals is, in general, less likely to pose problems than sponsorship of medical research. This is because the control of the educational process and content is more firmly in the hands of the educators who are usually not agents of the sponsors.

The commercial sponsorship of public health education is however much more worrying. Accurate, comprehensive and comprehensible health education is vitally important. Such education can come from commercial, voluntary or public sources. However there is a danger that information directly from, or sponsored by, commercial sources may be biased or incomplete.

State health provision including the production of health education materials will continue to suffer from financial restrictions and it is not realistic to ban commercial health education materials or to expect health professionals and teachers to refuse to use them. An accreditation scheme for all health education materials, including those sponsored by commercial concerns, would help to raise standards and current proposals for such a scheme are described below.

The Health Education Authority has a particular responsibility to be, and be seen to be, an impartial commentator on health issues. To ally themselves with food producers puts that position in peril.

Charities also have a duty to retain their position of impartiality. They too should avoid too close an association with commercial agencies who have a financial interest in health matters. Some charities, such as the Coronary Prevention Group, have a policy of refusing donations from such bodies despite relatively huge sums of money being offered. Once a charity loses its credibility it is very difficult to win it back. Furthermore, the actions of a few charities could undermine the reputation of the many. It will be to the detriment of the charitable sector as a whole if some charities are seen to become a marketing arm of large companies through sponsorship and endorsements. It is particularly important that charities do not allow themselves to become the route whereby the pharmaceutical industry gets round the law forbidding them to communicate directly with the public.

The Charity Commission should consider whether such sponsorship arrangements are truly 'charitable' and whether they pose a threat to the future of this sector. The Commission should also consider whether a code on accepting sponsorship should be introduced.

Service provision

While the provision of consumables such as diaries, pens, memo pads and so on by commercial sponsors is commonplace, examples of sponsorship of the direct delivery of medical care are now rare. There are some exceptions; firstly innovative areas of health care are sometimes sponsored. A recent report revealed that around a quarter of the 380 specialist 'stoma' nurses in Britain are privately funded by companies making stoma appliances. Stoma nurses advise patients who have had a colostomy (an opening from the colon), an ileostomy (from the small intestine), or a urostomy (from the urinary tract), about the appropriate bags, tubes, etc, to use.

Secondly, sponsorship is relatively common where an increase in services might lead to drug prescriptions. Screening for diseases which if detected may involve drug treatment is a prime candidate for this type of funding. For example, a recent government report noted that 'in Britain considerable interest is being generated in cholesterol testing by commercial companies, including those involved in the sale of desk-top measuring instrument and those involved in the manufacture of cholesterol lowering drugs...Commercial activity by pharmaceutical companies includes organising regional, national and international workshops and conferences and funding for 'Coronary Nurse Facilitators' who help primary care teams to establish blood cholesterol testing programmes. It is common practice for general practitioners to be lent desk-top testing machines by the pharmaceutical industry for limited periods during which they invite patients to be tested.'

Discussion

As with sponsorship of health education materials the sponsorship of medical care may lead to a deterioration in the quality of the service in some cases. For example, the sponsorship of stoma nurses may affect the advice given by those nurses. Kenneth Hargreaves, speaking for the Campaign for Impartial Stomacare in the *Guardian*, has pointed out that such sponsorship might be acceptable if the nurses were free to recommend other manufacturers' products, but he feared that this was not always the case. There have been reports of nurses being afraid that they might lose their job if they failed to increase sales of the sponsor's products, and in at least one case a patient was left in pain because a sponsored nurse refused to change an appliance to a rival firm's model even though it would have been more suitable.

The London *Evening Standard* recently reported that the Secretary of State for Health is considering inviting private food retailers, such as Safeways and Tescos to build new hospitals at their own expense in return for the old hospital buildings and any adjoining land. Commercial sponsors are likely to develop lucrative out-of-town sites rather than refurbish run-down innner-city hospitals. Patients may then have to travel long distances for the medical treatment they need while their local hospital deteriorates.

Controls on sponsorship

In comparison with other country's systems for control of sponsorship, the UK tends to rely more on self regulation and voluntary agreements than on strict and detailed legislation. It remains to be seen whether the voluntaristic elements will remain as the UK becomes more integrated with other European markets where this form of control is rarer. However there are some laws which control advertising and promotion. For example the 1990 Food Act and the 1984 Food Labelling Regulations cover food advertising and labelling. The 1968 Medicines Act and the 1978 Medicines (Labelling and Advertising to the Public) Regulations cover drugs. In addition various voluntary codes of practice apply – the Advertising Standards Authority covers advertising in the print media, and the Independent Television Commission is responsible for advertising on television.

The Code of Practice for the Pharmaceutical Industry administered by the Association of the British Pharmaceutical Industry regulates the promotion of drugs to the medical profession. The code specifies that: 'No gift or financial inducement shall be offered or given to members of the medical profession for the purpose of sales promotion' but exempts gifts which are 'inexpensive and relevant to the practice of medicine'. A recent survey came up with the following: a 'slinky spring' (to promote 'Mobilex'); a tube of Mexican jumping beans; plastic hip, shoulder and knee joints; a claret glass (advertising 'Clarityn'); and a pop-up Mad Hatter's Tea Party

There has been increasing concern in recent years about the relationship between health professionals and the pharmaceutical industry. Doctors spend large sums of public money on drugs for their patients with fewer restrictions than in almost any other area of public expenditure. Doctors are expected to prescribe these drugs on the basis of what they know about their appropriateness, efficacy and safety. It is generally recognised that there should be no suspicion that they are influenced by the receipt of gifts, hospitality or payments from pharmaceutical companies. That this concern is widely shared is apparent from recommendations made in various codes of practice for health professionals. For example the code of practice of the General Medical Council states that 'doctors should avoid accepting any pecuniary or material inducement that might compromise, or be regarded by others as likely to compromise, the independent exercise of their professional judgement in prescribing. The seeking or acceptance by doctors of unreasonable sums of money or gifts from commercial firms which manufacture or market drugs or diagnostic or therapeutic agents or appliances may be regarded as improper'.

In the absence of effective controls on sponsored health education materials it has recently been suggested by a working group convened by the Coronary Prevention Group that a national accreditation scheme for health education materials should be established. The Finnish Council for Health Education already operates such a scheme. Leaflets and other materials, from any source, are submitted to the scheme on a voluntary basis, and those found to meet the requisite standard are allowed to bear its stamp of approval. Health professionals using such materials know that they met certain standards. For a national scheme to operate successfully in the UK it would need to have the support of the government, charitable and commercial sectors.

Conclusion

Sponsorship is commonly thought of as the financial or other support by one agency of another's activity. On that broad definition sponsorship is everywhere. It has become an issue in recent years in a narrower sense because it is advertising by another name. There are legitimate concerns about sponsorship as advertising when considering the health sector. The economic and social importance of health makes those questions more critical than for other areas of sponsorship.

Most health sponsors have a direct economic interest in the activities they sponsor. As such, sponsorship in health offers opportunities for significant levels of funding, but also brings with it the possibility of unwelcome influences. We would all like the benefits without the cost but this ideal may not be attainable.

Therefore there is a need for vigilance on behalf of health professionals, stringent codes of conduct, and in some cases legislation, to maximise the benefits and minimise any abuses. It is not possible to separate commercial interests from health. It is difficult to imagine how, within a market economy, new drugs could be produced without the drug companies. However there are real dangers if the drug companies are allowed to act without strict supervision. Sponsorship should continue to be welcome but if in the words of a British Medical Association book on Medical Ethics, the treatment offered to the public is to be 'justified by its intrinsic merit, uninfluenced by commercial or financial interests' then controls need to be tight and well policed. When it comes to research on drugs the drug industry might dominate the stage but there is a continuing need for the Government and independent medical charities to fund research which may not have great commercial spin-offs.

Sponsorship of health education materials presents a similar challenge. Good materials are to be welcomed but there is a lack of controls to guarantee high standards. There is a role for the government here. Charities should look to their own role, maintain their independence and refuse sponsorship from organisations who have financial interests in areas where they have policy interests.

TIMOTHY LEGGATT

The Sponsorship of Television Programmes

Introduction

The sponsorship of television programmes in Great Britain is different from all other forms of sponsorship in the country in that it has only very recently become legal.

The BBC is prohibited by its Licence from broadcasting sponsored programmes and may not, without the prior approval of the Secretary of State, broadcast any advertising. In contrast, the commercial channels of Independent Television (ITV) have, since their beginnings, been almost wholly funded by advertising; and yet the first chapter of their former governing body's document concerning 'Advertising Rules and Practices (Television)' was entitled *No Sponsorship*. This indeed conveyed the spirit of all Broadcasting Acts before that of 1990.

The ITV regulatory body, the Independent Broadcasting Authority (IBA), was replaced under the 1990 Broadcasting Act, as a consequence of the Government's wish, in the prevailing technological, commercial and political circumstances of the late 1980s, to deregulate the airwaves and maximise the opportunities for 'market forces'. At the end of 1990 the IBA ceased to exist, and was replaced by the Independent Television Commission (ITC).

However, in the last year of its life, the IBA did relax its prohibition on programme sponsorship, to allow the sponsorship of the weather forecast, sports programmes and arts review programmes. Finally, effective from 1st January 1991, the ITC issued *The ITC Code of Programme Sponsorship*, which seeks not to prohibit, but to permit, sponsorship.

Under the ITC Code, with certain specified exceptions, any programme broadcast over ITV channels (Channels 3, 4 and 5) or by satellite channels up-linked from the UK or delivered by cable may be sponsored. The important exceptions are news and current affairs programmes and business and financial reports.

The background of regulation

Thus, television programme sponsorship in the UK is governed by regulation, whose justification lies in an Act of Parliament, the Broadcasting Act 1990.

However, the legislature is not free to abandon regulation, to promote a rampant free market in programme sponsorship, should it be so inclined; for behind the national legislation stands the directive of the Council of the European Communities, concerning the pursuit of television broadcasting activities, promulgated on 3rd October 1989 and from 3rd October 1991 effective in all Member States. And shadowing that document, with almost identical provisions concerning television sponsorship, is the Council of Europe's *Convention on Transfrontier Television*, which will, in due course, become binding on a yet larger number of European countries.

It is at this point that definitions become important, to provide a common understanding for the remainder of this chapter. The definition of programme sponsorship under the ITC Code is the following:

> A programme is deemed to be sponsored if any part of its costs of production or transmission is met by an organisation or person other than a broadcaster or television producer, with a view to promoting its own or another's name, trademark, image, activities, products or other direct or indirect commercial interests.

This definition is quite explicitly based on that of the EC Council's directive, which reads:

> 'sponsorship' means any contribution made by a public or private undertaking not engaged in television broadcasting activities or in the production of audio-visual works, to the financing of television programmes with a view to promoting its name, its trademark, its image, its activities or its products.

The contrast with advertising, while not overly sharp, is made by the Council in its statement that,

> 'television advertising' means any form of announcement broadcast in return for payment or for similar consideration by a public or private undertaking in connection with a trade, business, craft or profession in order to promote the supply of goods or services, including immovable property, or rights and obligations, in return for payment.

There are six basic rules concerning sponsorship laid down in the EC Council's Directive, which have become enshrined or strengthened in the ITC Code. Both the rules and the ITC's reaction to them have been vividly described in a paper by Frank Willis of the ITC, which is heavily drawn upon in the presentation which follows.[1]

'The *first* European rule,' writes Willis, 'is about safeguarding editorial independence: 'the content and scheduling of sponsored programmes may in no circumstances be influenced by the sponsor

in such a way as to affect the responsibility and editorial independence of the broadcaster in respect of programmes'. The ITC Code
states even more directly, 'No sponsor is permitted *any* influence
on either the content or the scheduling of a programme'.

Willis comments, 'The central philosophy of the Code is that
sponsorship is an arm's length partnership of mutual benefit. The
sponsor gets corporate or brand image benefit from a visible association with a particular programme. What he does *not* get is the
ability to influence editorial content or to use programme content
to promote advertising or other corporate needs.'

'The *second* European rule is about transparency: Sponsored
programmes "must be clearly identified as such by the name and/
or logo of the sponsor at the beginning and/or the end of the
programmes".'

Here Willis comments, 'Some people argue that this is the only
rule you need. Provided the viewers know who is paying, they can
form their own judgement of how much to believe...This is *not*
the philosophy of the Directive nor that of the ITC Code. Transparency should be seen not as a substitute for the principle of
non-interference in editorial, but as reinforcing it. If interference
is taking place, it is more likely to be detected if the potential
interferer is publicly identified.'

The ITC Code explicitly allows 'break bumper credits' (those
around the commercial breaks) but no credits within the programmes themselves – with limited exceptions for game shows and
coverage of sponsored events.

The *third* European rule prohibits promotional references. Sponsored programmes 'must not encourage the purchase or rental of
the products or services of the sponsor or a third party, in particular by making special promotional references to those products or
services'.

The ITC takes the view, in Willis's words, 'that the sponsor,
while an honoured and welcome guest in the credits, really has no
business popping up in the programme itself in *any* guise whatsoever. So no presenter T shirts, etc.' Nonetheless, there is difficulty in distinguishing between 'corporate slogans which might be
permitted and advertising slogans which clearly are not permitted'.

Willis continues, 'The ITC has not so far been satisfied that
this distinction can be sufficiently clearly defined. Rather than
promulgate a rule which would be endlessly disputed, we decided
to maintain an even playing field by outlawing promotional slogans
of any kind from sponsor credits...But we are continuing to listen

to suggestions for tackling this point differently, and I would not altogether rule out the possibility of some movement...'

The *fourth* European rule aims to prevent sponsorship by prohibited advertisers: 'Television programmes may not be sponsored by natural or legal persons whose principal activity is the manufacture or sale of products, or the provision of services, the advertising of which is prohibited by Article 13 (tobacco) or 14 (prescription drugs).'

The ITC takes the view that prohibited advertisers are also prohibited sponsors, but, notes Willis, 'the ITC has been able to preserve discretion to look at particular cases on their merits'.

The *fifth* European rule, in Willis's words, 'puts a ring fence round news and current affairs programmes: "News and current affairs programmes may not be sponsored". The rationale is that even if the sponsor does not actively interfere, the programme maker will pull his punches if a topic comes up which does not suit the sponsor's interest – be it a share scandal, environmental criticism or a product safety scare.'

The ITC Code strengthens this provision by forbidding sponsorship in any circumstances where, had a programme not been sponsored, 'it might reasonably have been expected to contain editorial content which might conflict with the sponsor's interest'.

The *sixth* and last European rule restricts product placement. The Council of Europe Convention (which in this case is clearer that the EC Directive) states: 'Surreptitious advertisements shall not be allowed, in particular the presentation of products and services in programmes when it serves advertising purposes'.

As Willis comments, 'This is something of a regulatory minefield and the ITC Code picks its way with care. It does not forbid absolutely the free supply of branded products for use by a programme maker, but insists that this must be confined to cases where they are an essential element in the programme, and then only provided 'no undue prominence' is given to them. In no circumstances may programme makers accept payment, in cash or kind, for the inclusion of products, and it follows that deals where the nature and duration of the product's appearance are negotiated are also outlawed.'

The ITC has the task of monitoring and policing the observance of its Code of regulations by broadcasters, which in this area could become problematic. Nonetheless, Willis concludes, 'The ITC may not be able to prevent irregular product placement in advance, but it will have swingeing retrospective sanctions at its disposal. From 1993 it will be able to fine a Channel 3 licensee up to 3% of its advertising and sponsorship revenue for a first offence and up to 5% for a second offence. With that potential firepower it will not be difficult to fit the punishment to the crime.'

The ITC Code is widely said not to be sufficiently clear, which has led to much time and attention being paid to issues of interpretation. It is also criticised for being too restrictive. This means that there will continue to be pressure brought to bear on the ITC, as we shall see below, to make the Code more permissive.

Nonetheless, this presentation of the European rules will serve to remind the reader of something that many commentators evidently forget, that there are limits, agreed by the British government and its close partners in Europe, to the freedoms which television programme sponsors may be allowed.

The start of sponsorship affecting British viewers

The beginning of television programme sponsorship for UK viewers came with the first Sky Channel going on air, with signals from continental Europe, in 1982, followed by Super Channel five years later. The start is vividly described by John Marchant,[2] who then worked for Super Channel, as follows:

> What really happened was that the European broadcasters had immense regulations, even more than in this country, so the satellite gave the advertisers an opportunity to say, 'This is a new medium, for some of you; and not only that but there's another way of doing it apart from spot airtime, and it's called sponsorship'. In the early days, Sky Channel and Super Channel's revenues were made up, nearly up to 50%, of sponsorship revenue – coming from sponsorship related matters.
>
> Really what clients were doing was experimenting, because the entry price was cheap and they could see what they did right and what they did wrong. The traditional boys came in, like CocaCola and Pepsi and Mobil and Shell, but also a lot of Japanese clients came in – because sponsorship is normal in Japan; every other programme is sponsored on Japanese television. They gave their brand managers in Europe the go-ahead – 'Get on with it, because we've done it at home and it works. Let's see how they do it in Europe; and let's gain a foothold before the terrestrial broadcasters come up to speed'. That's really how it all developed.

But, naturally, most viewers did not see this development. The signal for the start of sponsorship on terrestrial channels in Britain did not come until late in 1988 with the publication of the Broadcasting Bill. Then, in the spring of 1989, the IBA ended its 'No sponsorship' policy, and permitted sponsorship of weather reports, instructional and arts review programmes and the coverage of events, such as sporting events, provided that they were not specifically created for television. This was the change that prompted the ITV companies and Channel 4 to consider whether or not they wished to move into the sponsorship arena.

In 1989 a number of regional programmes were sponsored, for example, Heinecken sponsored an ice hockey event for Granada. The first network show to be sponsored was *Pets and People*, sponsored by Pedigree Petfoods, also for Granada. This sponsorship became controversial, and was stopped, when the IBA took the view that the link between sponsor and programme content was too close for editorial integrity to be guaranteed. Finally, in September 1989 came the first national sponsorship of which most British viewers were aware, the sponsorship of the national weather forecast by PowerGen, the newly floated, private electricity generating company.

This was inevitably a period of slow movement, a period of transition between the IBA's 'No sponsorship' policy and the development of the new ITC Code. In 1990, PowerGen renewed its contract with ITV (to 1992) and its fellow generating company, National Power, established its name through sponsorship of British television coverage of the football World Cup competition.

Then, in January 1991, the ITC came into existence, together with *The ITC Code of Programme Sponsorship*.

The development of programme sponsorship

The sponsors' story

The views of firms that have actively explored the possibilities of television programme sponsorship have been tapped through a series of interviews, carried out with representatives of Croft Port, Lloyds Bank, National Power, PowerGen and Sony. All these companies have sponsored nationally viewed television programmes shown on ITV or – in the case of Lloyds Bank – a televised event for which the BBC provides broadcast coverage.

PowerGen and the National Weather Reports, 1989-91

PowerGen[3] and National Power are the two new electricity generating companies that were created as a result of the privatising of the Central Electricity Generating Board in 1990. The companies had not existed before the privatisation of the CEGB and they were to be floated on the Stock Exchange, with shares offered to the public at large.

PowerGen perceived the critical public relations task to be that of creating awareness of the company. To achieve this, they wished to do something that was informative but also innovative and unusual. In April 1989, therefore, they put in their bid for somewhat under £2 million – alongside several other companies – to sponsor for one year the national weather report that follows the ITN news. They won the sponsorship, which went on air in September 1989.

By February 1990 research showed that spontaneous public awareness of the company had reached 37%, and prompted awareness nearly 60%. However, the official flotation was still some months off and PowerGen decided to continue with the sponsorship, to increase the company's name awareness. They secured a second sponsorship contract for a further two and a quarter years at a cost of just under £4 million; and this time they built into the sponsorship other activities, such as running competitions in schools.

PowerGen have been well satisfied. They concluded the first national sponsorship deal. They believe that their shareholders, customers and employees have all benefited – the last group through knowing that they work for a company that is not stuffy and is thoughtful about its advertising expenditure. They consider that the sponsorship 'fits', since the weather is related to the need to generate electricity and the weather report is seen by everyone. It has achieved what they wished it to achieve.

PowerGen is clear that programme sponsorship is akin to advertising rather than philanthropy, such as sponsorship of the local boys' football team; but it is much less expensive, in terms of the cost of airtime. In PowerGen's case the money for sponsorship is new, that is, the budget for it is separate from the advertising budget.

National Power and the Football World Cup, 1990

National Power[4] is bigger than PowerGen (the size ratio is 5:3), but it was second in launching its awareness campaign. Coming second, it too felt the need to do something distinctive. Fortunately, the Football World Cup, the major sporting event of 1990, provided a new and special opportunity for programme sponsorship, for which National Power proceeded to negotiate. It secured the sponsorship contract and a valuable, concentrated period for promoting both awareness of its name and a statement about the company, that they are the largest electricity generator in the country.

For £2 million the company bought approximately 70 hours of exposure, and they supplemented the sponsorship by working with the local press and local radio, running competitions and joining in events – all to increase people's knowledge of National Power. They ran a continuous tracking study, to gauge awareness of the company, awareness of what it did and attitudes towards it; and on all measures their ratings increased to their satisfaction.

National Power also considers that the cost of sponsorship is not great, when compared with advertising; and believes that the increasing fragmentation of television (as a result of the development of cable and satellite channels) may lead more companies to concentrate on sponsorship at the expense of advertising. Thus, the money going into programme sponsorship may be expected to be a mixture of old and new, in other words, from advertising budgets and from new sponsorship budgets.

Sony and the Rugby World Cup, 1991

The interest of Sony[5] in television sponsorship is not, of course, to promote awareness of the name, for the only brand name that is better known throughout the world, according to Sony, is Coca Cola. What Sony sought in sponsoring the Rugby World Cup in 1991 was much more specific: image enhancement among a targeted audience of potential buyers, those known in advertising circles as ABC1 men.

Thus, Sony bought a property – 73 hours of World Cup rugby – which delivered an audience that normal advertising finds very elusive and has great difficulty in targeting precisely. But beyond access to this target audience, Sony also bought an association which the company believed offered image enhancement. Rugby, they argued, is an amateur sport (just) and it is played for fun; and likewise, Sony products, which are 'consumer leisure goods' and not necessities, are bought for fun, for enjoyment. In this way, the fit was considered to be good.

The contract gave Sony break-bumpers, which the company used for the 'Sony Rugby Trivia Quiz': for the 200 breaks in the broadcast coverage they invited a panel of experts to compose 200 trivial questions about rugby football throughout the world. The aim was for liveliness and fun – another opportunity to enhance the Sony image. Finally, the cost of £2 million broke down between £1.7 million paid to ITV for the sponsorship and £300,000 given to Rugby World Cup Ltd, which gave Sony a 'good neighbour', philanthropic, opportunity.

In Sony's view, more commercial revenue is going into television as a result of the sponsorship opportunity. Many companies want to have major exposure and sponsorship provides a not too expensive way. The need is to find 'the right programme' to sponsor, through which to reach 'the right audience'.

Croft Port and 'Rumpole of the Bailey', from 1991

Croft Port,[6] a subsidiary of International Distillers & Vintners (IDV), was the final pioneer of 1991 in the sponsorship arena. It was the first sponsor in this country of a drama series, indeed of any drama programme.

In the market for port, Crofts are leaders of a small group of firms (which includes Taylors, Grahams and Dow) at the premium end of the market. In earlier years they promoted their product with a concentrated, ten-week, black and white press advertising campaign in the period leading up to Christmas. In 1991, however, they broke with tradition by moving into television, with sponsorship of a new six-week series of a well-loved classic, *Rumpole of the Bailey*, by John Mortimer.

For a fee of £300,000, Thames Television offered Crofts: 15 seconds of opening credits, with a voiceover, which merged smoothly into the established opening credits for *Rumpole*; break-bumpers which showed, at the start of each commercial break, a port-coloured wash disappearing downwards from the screen and, at the close of the break, a similar wash filling the screen from the bottom up; and 15 seconds of closing credits, with voiceover, that showed an empty wine glass being put down on a table.

But what they bought on the nation's television screens was emphatically not mere time, such as commercial breaks offer advertisers every day. Far more than this, it was an association – with the character played by Leo McKern, the crusty barrister, Horace Rumpole. In the words of Crofts' spokesman, 'He's a bit of an institution. It all smacks of heritage and quality.' Put in another way, Croft Port sought to enhance its image and that of its product through an association with the image of a well-established television programme.

However, as Crofts well knew, that was still ·not all. They also bought an opportunity for further, linked promotion, uncontrolled by any regulation. They organised a great deal of trade promotion: they linked themselves with Penguin's publication of the book of the series, *Rumpole à la Carte*; and they put on sale a quarter of a million bottles of port in retail outlets with a special offer attached.

That was planned, and represents the kind of opportunity that a well-chosen sponsorship can make available. In Crofts' particular case there were yet further benefits beyond those expected, namely, very generous press coverage of this new television sponsorship initiative. It has been suggested that the cost of the press coverage, had it had to be bought, would have exceeded the fee paid to ITV.

It has been commented that the fit between Croft Port and *Rumpole* is unusually and peculiarly good – perhaps especially because the character portrayed drinks claret and not port, which would have been too close for the comfort of all concerned. Another view is that there are many more equally suitable associations to be found, if only those who seek them search hard and long enough.

Lloyds Bank and the BBC Young Musician of the Year, from 1992

The sponsorship by Lloyds Bank[7] of the *Young Musician of the Year* competition and Masterclasses is a kind of sponsorship distinct from those so far discussed. It is the sponsorship of events rather than of programmes, which the BBC cannot accept under the terms of its Licence.

Nonetheless, while to the BBC this is *event sponsorship* (and thus allowable), from Lloyds' perspective it is *TV sponsorship*. It is so described in their relevant press release and, it seems, entirely appropriately.

Lloyds Bank is providing £1.3 million sponsorship over five years 'to enhance and develop Britain's premiere musical event for young people, the BBC Young Musician of the Year'. The reward is that each of 15 programmes in the appropriate year (the competition is run every two years) will carry references – two verbal mentions and a visual credit – to Lloyds Bank's sponsorship. For these programmes the audience is estimated (on past years' experience) to cumulate to 20 million over the three month period; and, furthermore, it has an AB index of 190, which compares excellently with sport's ability to reach this target audience. Badminton, the leading sport on this index, scores 153.

So, from Lloyds' viewpoint the audience is highly rated in terms of quality as well as quantity. But Lloyds – very like Croft Port – has secured more than references. It is associating itself, on the one hand, with the quality and excellence for which the BBC is still held in high regard and, on the other, with young people engaged in the pursuit of similar standards of achievement. And it has the right to declare and advertise this association in each of its 2,000 branches throughout the country.

This particular sponsorship fits into a broad strategy, pursued by Lloyds, of sponsoring activities associated with young people, with the objective of 'enhancing the Bank's image to this important market'. It is seen as complementing the Lloyds Bank Theatre Challenge and the Lloyds Bank Fashion Challenge in projecting the bank as 'modern, friendly and accessible'.

Lloyds is well content with this sponsorship. Commissioned research in 1991 showed that 82% of those approached agree that this is a suitable and worthwhile event for Lloyds Bank to sponsor. Lloyds therefore believes that their sponsorship is understood, that their customers are comfortable with it and their employees proud of it, and that they have found an appropriate niche for themselves in the sponsorship field.

In assessing the venture, Lloyds' spokesman, David Goldesgeyme, said, 'It's difficult to be able to say that sponsorship is worth so much in terms of its benefits, in relation to what you're paying for it. You don't just get a £ sign.' Yet, in comparison with advertising, 'We're getting much closer to the hearts and minds of people through sponsorship.'

Lloyds sees the benefits as mutual. The sponsorship, comments Goldesgeyme, 'gives the BBC a profile, it gives their programme a profile. The BBC gets the advantage of our 2,000 branches, which the BBC doesn't have. That has a real advantage for the BBC, as does the image of Lloyds Bank. That's an interesting area for the BBC to consider: what does the sponsor bring to the party, apart from money?'

The broadcasters' perspective

Although we have begun this examination of the development of television sponsorship by looking at the sponsors' side of the business, it is of course the broadcasters, and only the broadcasters, who can authorise a sponsorship agreement. We now therefore look at the approaches to sponsorship of four representative ITV companies – Granada Television, London Weekend Television (LWT), Scottish Television and Thames Television, Channel 4 and the BBC.

Granada Television

Of the television executives seen in the course of research for this chapter, John Marchant of Granada has the longest experience of sponsorship. He joined Granada in late 1988, having previously been involved with sponsorship at Super Channel and even earlier at Capital Radio. He knows well the history of television sponsorship and has been involved with many of the early sponsorship deals – with Heinecken, Pedigree Petfoods, National Power and Sony, among others.

He sees sponsorship as having developed as a natural evolution, as the ITV companies realised, following publication of the 1988 Broadcasting Bill, that they would have to share the advertising cake with new satellite companies, so that they needed to find other ways of raising money. With the Sony and Croft Port sponsorships, in Marchant's words, 'we're starting to see the creative evolution of this movement...because what people have to remember about television is that viewers do not have channel loyalty, they have programme loyalty. They don't really give a damn what channel (a programme is) on, but what they do have is massive programme loyalty, which is where sponsorship has a major plus... So, sponsorship has now come of age.'

Here then are Marchant's predictions for the future, to which we shall return at the conclusion of the chapter.

1. Satellite and cable channels only came under ITC regulations on 1st October 1991, and Marchant believed that this would result in pressure on the ITC for some relaxation of the Code. Probably, they will give Sky and cable companies and satellite companies a slight edge in terms of what they can do.

2. While expenditure on sponsorship will never amount to more than 10% of expenditure on advertising, that is still £150 million.[8] This will not happen for quite some time and not unless there is some relaxation in the ITC rules.

3. In future there will be more co-productions – with advertisers rather than broadcasters. 'Traditionally we've always done them with another broadcaster and they will continue to be done. With another broadcaster you get a creative problem – who really has control? Whereas if you do a co-production with an advertiser, he tends to let you have creative control. He's coming to you for your expertise...But it won't happen overnight.'

4. 'I can see in time, especially with big sports – a big fight or a big game, the network scheduler will go to someone and say, "can you get me sponsorship for this?" And that guy will make a few phone calls, and someone will say, "I'll back it"; and he'll go back and say, "you can bid this much, because I can provide this much money". But it isn't going to happen next week.'

5. 'Programme makers will be anxious about editorial integrity till their dying day, because it's their **art**; whereas I treat it like a product. But less and less and less are they worried about editorial influence. They're more worried about the look of it. So, the issue is, "how are we going to work together to get something that looks right, looks smart, has a synergistic feel?" In that, ITV has the final say on what goes out on air.'

6. 'Our problem is scheduling. In the future we should go to an advertiser and say, "We are thinking of making *Maigret* with Michael Gambon, and we need a sponsor. Does this interest you?" He will say, "yes, if I can run a promotion which I can plan and budget for 18 months in advance, within my 5 year plan". He would have enough time to be able to exploit the opportunities. Whereas now we're saying, "*Maigret* is on in three months' time".'

In sum, in Marchant's view, *in the long term* the regulations will be relaxed, there will be much more programme sponsorship – possibly as much as the equivalent, in 1991 terms, of 75 Rugby World Cup deals each year (or 450 *Rumpole* deals) and there will be advertisers' money going directly into programme production. At the same time, the broadcasters' editorial control will be maintained and the whole sponsorship scene will be better managed to make possible the long term planning that all parties require.

London Weekend Television (LWT)

Richard Holliday,[9] our informant at LWT, spoke at length about the transition that has had to take place within the ITV companies from an age of public service broadcasting to a more commercial age. In his words, 'the whole sponsorship debate is wrapped up with prejudices that people have as a result of Reithian broadcasting and how the BBC was organised and *therefore* the way the ITV structure was organised – the mirror image of the BBC, except that it's funded differently'. That background has made the introduction of a new cost culture, a new commercial culture, difficult and slow. But it has had to come. 'Quite clearly the companies are being encouraged to behave as commercial organisations with a proper profit ethos.'

Holliday strongly emphasised the difference between the ITV system and the commercial broadcasting system of the USA. 'Our system is completely different. We start with public service broadcasting, firstly funded by the licence fee, then funded by advertising. Politicians in the 50s were worried about what had happened in

America, and every safeguard was built into the Broadcasting Act
to prevent any kind of incursion into editorial influence, to create
insulation between the artistic side of the business and the financial
side. The politicians saw ITV as *public service broadcasting being
sponsored by commercial enterprise.'* (author's emphasis)

What is new, following the 1990 Broadcasting Act, is the emphasis on programmes; and here Holliday agrees with Marchant, 'In
the end delivery systems aren't the thing that's important, the thing
that's important are programmes'. With sponsorship, a commercial is
no longer insulated, it 'is being attached to a programme. And the
added value and benefit is already inherent within the programme.'

This is why appropriateness or fit is so important. In Holliday's
words, 'A programme has a very strong and powerful brand identity. There is already a brand value for the programme, a brand
value that has been built up very carefully by the programme
makers. They're very keen to satisfy their customers and their
peer group as well.' It is this that advertisers and their agents
have to appreciate and build their sponsorship strategies around.
This is 'a new communication opportunity, which is clearly very
powerful'.

Holliday's vision of the future is more cautious than Marchant's,
but he too foresees an increase in sponsorship and sponsorship
funds going straight into programme production. He predicts:

1. If two peaktime programmes were sponsored each day on the
ITV network for 52 weeks in the year, it would be worth about
£32 million. 'I don't think that sponsorship in 1993 is going to be
worth more than £30 million.'

2. Possibly five programmes a night could be sponsored (worth
about £80 million), not necessarily produced by producer-broad-
casters but acquired by publisher-broadcasters. But 'I can't see a
situation where programmes or television companies are going to
be funded by sponsorship to a degree that makes it of any massive
importance'.

3. 'The one area that I think could be interesting is sport. Sport
needs television just as much as television needs sport. In the US
the package is put together by somebody on behalf of the television
company; the television rights are everything. Without the television
rights, the whole thing is dead. We're going to be saying, "we don't
just want the broadcasting rights".'

4. Advertiser-funded programmes are bound to come. 'The
central scheduler may have £600 million to spend. If someone
comes along with an advertiser-funded very high quality programme,

it's going to be very difficult to turn it down. Who will then be in control?'

Scottish Television (STV) and the Independent Television Association (ITVA)

Alan Chilton[10] claims for Scottish Television a number of pioneering sponsorship achievements. They were the first ITV company to obtain a sponsor for their regional weather reports – Kwik-fit in 1990; the first to find a sponsor for a British soap opera – Brook Bond (Unilever) for *Take the High Road* or a children's programme – the Bank of Scotland's Young Savers' Scheme for Glen Michael's *Cartoon Cavalcade*; and the first to find a sponsor for a business programme – Scottish Enterprise for a business game, 'to create an interest in Scottish business'.

It is a striking record, of raising £750,000 from sponsors, for which the equivalent for the whole ITV network would be of the order of £13 million. Chilton conceded that the quest for sponsorship was helped by the fact that Scotland is a nation, as well as being a region, so that he has 'a lot of blue chip advertisers to call upon'.

Chilton became Chairman of the ITVA Sponsorship Committee in 1991, and could therefore speak also on behalf of the ITVA. The concern, he said, was that sponsorship might dilute the effectiveness of spot advertising, upon which the ITV companies are totally dependent; and the other worry was viewer irritation. But, in contrast to the US situation, 'in this country there's a very positive attitude towards TV advertising. It's more creative, there's considerably less of it, it's less intrusive.'

Chilton was optimistic about the future. He expected the ITC regulations to be further relaxed, for example, to allow sponsorship in support of national promotions of the kind offered by oil companies. And perhaps television would get into event sponsorship – such as domestic football as Sky has done. He foresaw co-productions but not barter, since its development in the US was due to the disproportion between the amount of airtime that there was to fill (on 200 channels) and the amount of available programming.

He predicted steady growth in the revenue derived from sponsorship: maybe £20 million in 1993, maybe £35 million in 1994, perhaps £50 million in the mid-1990s. But 'if it ever got to more than 2-3% of spot advertising revenue (in 1990 terms, £35-£52 million), I'd be surprised'.

Thames Television

Tim Brady[11] at Thames Television has a fine record of attracting sponsorship. He secured the *Evening Standard's* sponsorship of *01*, Croft Port's of *Rumpole of the Bailey* and Barclaycard's sponsorship of *Wish You Were Here*.

He commented, however, that it had not been an easy market. Much time had been spent in lobbying the IBA about the regulations. And people on the programme side thought that sponsorship meant 'trespassing' in their area. Although the income from sponsorship went into a central pool, 'they still greet you with a huge amount of suspicion'.

Only a few advertising agencies have taken sponsorship seriously. 'Everybody thinks we're fending people off', but it has not been like that. Partly, no doubt, this is due to the recession, but also, for 1991, the ITV was too late in naming programmes considered suitable for sponsorship. And they were not imaginative: why were all the listed programmes at peaktime and why were no children's programmes offered? It was vital to identify suitable programmes and to be proactive about them.

He was cautious about the future. 'Sponsorship will always be small relative to airtime (advertising). A deal of £1 million is good. How can people say that sponsorship to the amount of £80 million is likely?'

Channel 4

Stewart Butterfield, Channel 4's Director of Advertising Sales and Marketing, found much confusion about sponsorship when he joined Channel 4 in early 1991 – 'there was a lot of worry about compromising the channel and the programmes'.[12]

However, within weeks 'we decided that the clash between editorial integrity and commercial gain could be rationalised, could actually fit together'; and Channel 4 produced its own Code of Programme Sponsorship. This stated as a basic principle that 'the editorial integrity of the channel's output is key to its success'. It is somewhat *more* restrictive than the ITC Code, adding documentaries and consumer information programmes (for example, on business, travel or gardening) to the programmes that may not be sponsored. Also, 'C4 still keeps the right to reject sponsorship for individual programmes on the basis of unsuitability.'

Sponsorship is seen as a source of income for the channel, like advertising, and not as a subsidy for production. The Channel 4 Code states expressly that 'no negotiation or agreement between a production house and sponsor will be acceptable to the channel'. This is because variety is part of the mission of the channel and this could be compromised, given that certain types of programmes are more likely to attract sponsorship than others. 'So the commissioning process has to take no account whatsoever of sponsorship.' A list is drawn up of the programmes thought to be most sellable 'and then the sales force (an outside firm) will go out and find sponsorship from potential advertisers'.

Butterfield felt that most potential sponsors had not yet understood what programme sponsorship is about. 'The real skill of the programme sponsor is the exploitation of their end of the product. If you sponsor a programme, you should be using that property in terms of promotions and competitions and ongoing activities. Simply sticking your name at the beginning and end of a programme doesn't achieve very much, to my mind. But that means resource, and many clients don't have that. It means ingenuity beyond normal, traditional marketing.' And of agencies he commented, 'Most agencies haven't yet made that jump, to see sponsorship as another form of communication'.

As to the future, 'I've been quoted as saying that I expect 2% of our income to come from sponsorship. I may well be right or wrong. Advertising is 96% of the revenue of the channel. I don't think it's going to be a major source of funds'.

The BBC

Patricia Hodgson, Head of the Policy and Planning Unit at the BBC, set out the BBC's position with great clarity.[13]

> The starting point is a straightforward one, that Clause 12 of the Licence is a total prohibition on sponsorship. It says that the BBC 'may not take advertising without the agreement of the Home Secretary, and shall not take sponsorship'.
> Then the complications begin to arise, because the BBC inevitably, for good editorial reasons, wishes to cover major events, usually sporting events, which involve the sponsorship business. Then you have to start having rules and regulations to keep the sponsor at arm's length from the BBC and dealing only with the sporting body – and the sporting body actually getting all the benefit.
> So there is a long history of guidelines constricting the sponsorship messages surrounding the event: a limit to banners around the ground, an attempt, which has been long lost, to keep the sponsor's name out of titles of events, and a long rearguard action to limit the benefits that the sponsor gets on air; in other words, to try to prevent the fact that he's sponsoring the event – for which he deserves proper recognition, because he has put money into this public activity – from tipping over into advertising. A very, very difficult thing to do.

The economics of it, of course, are that the organisers of sporting events get an income from sponsors and do not need to charge the broadcasters so much for the right to cover the event. So at one remove, and indirectly, there is a trade-off. Broadcasters benefit.

Like any business activity the practice of sponsorship is dynamic, and this has led the BBC continually to reconsider its position. 'We don't want to be closed-minded or uninventive on our business side, in the way we conduct our affairs, so a lot of thought goes into this.' So the BBC puts aside scripted programmes, whether made on film or in the studio, where the creative input of the writer, the editor, the director or the producer can be recognised. 'There shall be no sponsorship involved in such programmes, because that must compromise the editorial integrity of the programme and, therefore, we can have nothing to do with that.'

However, the event area is different, and some years ago the BBC had discussions with the Home Office about it. These led to the following agreement:

> The sponsor of an artistic event or performance may pay the fees of the performers, including a fee to cover the cost of performing rights; and the BBC may then cover the performance, which is less expensive than it would otherwise have been, if the BBC had had to pay for the performing rights. There is mutual benefit, and it's consistent with the Licence, because the BBC is not receiving money from the sponsor.
>
> There is no editorial *infection*, because a performance has a self-contained existence, it is a public event. So we are not diverting the sponsorship money from the artistic world which is reliant on it, into broadcasting, which has its own discrete forms of funding. This should be a mutually beneficial arrangement. We still may not receive 'a valuable consideration' which helps to fund a programme.
>
> Further discussions with the Home Office have led to the advice that 'where a free-standing performance has been organised by the BBC, such as the Proms, it would be consistent with the Licence for a sponsor to defray the costs of the performance. And that enables us to have an agreement with Lloyds Bank to bolt on an extra dimension of performance to the *Young Musician of the Year.*
>
> Again, mutually beneficial. However, that is as far as, under the current Licence, we are permitted to go.

The nub of the issue for the BBC is the recognition that a sponsoring company usually wants 'some reflection of credit to its product or its corporate image', which means that 'a sponsor usually has an editorial angle, however tangential. That is obviously a matter of concern for the BBC.'

Hodgson believes that the issues will be looked at again when the BBC's Charter comes up for review in 1996 – 'with the benefit of the experience of ITV. By the time the review gets fully under way, ITV will have been trying to develop this market for some years and we'll have an idea of how much money there is in it and how it works.'

But it will do so cautiously, not only out of concern for editorial integrity but for three further reasons also. First is the issue of freedom of choice: 'would it mean that the choices made about what we showed would be confined? You know that sponsors are not going to sponsor difficult plays about AIDS victims and so on. That experience has been borne out time and time again in America.'

Second is the audience's perception of the BBC's independence: 'The BBC would have to ask itself, given that we get a compulsory licence fee to provide cultural coverage, for example, or drama, for the nation, what conclusions would people draw if, for some of what we did, the credit was associated with Mobil or BP or whoever?...It's not that the sponsor *has* actually perverted the programme; it's if the audience thinks they might have.'

Third is the matter of money. Would sponsorship undermine the argument for the licence fee? 'That wouldn't matter, of course, if there was sufficient sponsorship there to support your business as a cultural provider; but there isn't.' On Hodgson's calculation in 1990, which she has often made public and which has never been queried, the total sponsorship market was worth about £300 million at that time. Of that sum, about £5 million was going into television sponsorship.

With these points in mind, it seems highly unlikely that the BBC will change its present policy about programme sponsorship. The arguments against this will be just as relevant and valid, as 1996 approaches, as they are today.

The Specialised Agencies

The organisations with the liveliest interest and the greatest investment in the development of television sponsorship are those that have come into existence to promote it. For our purpose here, three such organisations will be considered: Media Dimensions, which exists to negotiate deals with broadcasters on behalf of would-be sponsors; Wood Lynds which works for broadcasters seeking sponsors for their programmes; and the Sponsorship Rating Company, which advises both sides about the price of sponsorship.

It can be no surprise that those who ride on the back of sponsorship see an exciting future for their mount and for other horses from the same stable.

Media Dimensions

An offshoot of the advertising agents, Young & Rubicam, Media Dimensions is an autonomous company established in early 1990 'to exploit the potential of a range of new communications opportunities in television'.[14] To date they have been exclusively concerned with television sponsorship.

Nick Bryant and Paul Green, directors of Media Dimensions, are eloquent about what they do. 'We see programme sponsorship as a brand new marketing tool, what we call "presence marketing". You are associating yourself with a programme – which is why people watch TV anyway – in a way you can't achieve by running an ad in a commercial break, where you're shoulder to shoulder with other advertisers. It's a completely different way of getting something across. It's not blatant. It's not a call to arms.'

Their first client was *The European*, for which they negotiated in 1990 the sponsorship of television coverage in the Soviet Union of the Soviet team playing an international match prior to the Football World Cup. They have also been involved in Zonephone's sponsorship in 1990 of the first local weather report on LWT; in the *Evening Standard's* sponsorship of *01* on Thames Television; in the insurance firm Legal & General's sponsorship in 1991 of the local weather reports on fourteen stations of the ITV network; and in Croft Port's sponsorship of *Rumpole of the Bailey* on the ITV network.

The Legal & General venture was a project on a grand scale, and an account of it will demonstrate the role of Media Dimensions in this field. 'In mid 1990 we approached Legal & General and proposed that they should sponsor the regional weather forecasts across the country. L&G had not been on television for over a year and without any high street shops or estate agencies to keep their name in front of the public, general awareness of their name was declining fast. The regional weather forecasts gave them the opportunity to achieve a very high profile in association with regional programming on a national basis.'

So their labours began. 'We had enormous problems with the IBA over the use of the logo; they wouldn't let us use it intact. There weren't any real guidelines and you couldn't use the logo and the name – it was one or the other. We finally got a compro-

mise, whereby we could sink the umbrella into the name so that
the & became part of the logo.' They then had to negotiate with
the ITV companies. 'We were working across fourteen different
stations, so that's fourteen different negotiations involving the
sponsorship executive at the station, the sales director, the director of programming, the director of local programming, the director of local presentation, the contracts department – on average
eight or nine different people at each station.'

What have they achieved? 'It's on every day, 365 days a year.
We cover every segment of the television audience, because it's on
at noon, three in the afternoon, five o'clock, the early news break,
the late news break. What we try to do in the creative treatment
is to put a bit of warmth and humour into it, because most people
perceive buying insurance as a distress purchase ('It costs a lot of
money, you never see it, but you've got to have it.'). No one's
overcome that with advertising, but we thought we could move
L&G away from that, give them a property that's completely
unique, that no one else can usurp, and create a bit of warmth. It's
an awareness campaign, to put L&G at the front of people's minds.'

The exact degree of success of this venture had yet to be ass-
essed by research, but it is evident that some considerable success
must have been achieved in terms of raising awareness of Legal &
General.

Developing programme sponsorship, in Bryant and Green's
eyes, has been 'a very uphill struggle with the broadcasters'.
However, with the path more or less mapped and the ITV franchise auction completed, there should now be growing interest
and 'much more co-operation from the stations in pushing back
the barriers'. They see arm's length sponsorship as only the first
of the 'new communications opportunities'. They predict, 'in the
future sponsorship will prime the pump for productions. If a production is going to cost a broadcaster less because it's got a sponsor riding in on it, a lot of broadcasters will greet that with open
arms. Advertiser-funded co-production is the next logical step,
and that's where the future lies.'

Wood Lynds

Wood Lynds is a sales agency, set up in April 1991, working for
organisations seeking sponsorship.[15] Among their clients have been
Channel 4, Screensport, Lifestyle and a number of independent
producers.

Developments have been slow, according to Mark Wood, one

of the managing partners. 'There hasn't been an influx of sponsors. No one is sure of the effects of sponsorship, what it does and how you can use it. And the broadcasters haven't got their act together, over how they should market sponsorship and what they can offer. But it's changing. About £12 million has been committed to sponsorship this year, twice the amount last year. There are 37 programmes offered by ITV for sponsorship next year. So about £30-40 million will be spent next year.'

National Power and PowerGen got into sponsorship to buy an awareness level. But most companies come to sponsorship 'for image – to preserve it or to change it'.

'Image is all, you're buying the values of the programme. Programme producers are brand managers of programmes and they have their own values, their own target audiences. All you're doing with sponsorship is trying to match your values with someone else's...It's going to be more significant, more sensitive and more important to get right than advertising. If you get sponsorship wrong, your image is affected. Sponsorship can be more powerful than advertising.'

The advice is clear. Programmes have values and audiences, which broadcasters may sell to would-be sponsors. They, in their turn, should therefore look for the right target audience and the values that fit their image or that they wish their image to fit. For both parties the match must be right.

Independent producers complicate the picture. 'In an ideal world the broadcaster commissions an independent producer to make a programme and the independent producer says what it is going to cost. Sometimes producers come up with a price that broadcasters can't afford, and then sponsors fill the gap.'

'Unfortunately,' comments Wood, 'Channel 4 don't want that to happen. They don't want any programme to be commissioned that is contingent upon finding sponsorship money to fill the budget gap, and they won't allow independent producers to do deals with sponsors direct.'

But Wood evidently foresees sponsorship money becoming more important – Channel 4 apart – as a subsidy for programme production.

The Sponsorship Rating Company

The Sponsorship Rating Company[16] was set up in 1991, to provide systematic evaluations of the price of sponsorship – in any medium. It therefore faces both ways. It offers potential sponsors a pre-purchase evaluation of a particular sponsorship – in terms of its uniqueness, its target audience, its consistency with the intended message, its overall match and so forth. It provides media owners with justification of the price or range of prices that they are asking for a sponsorship.

Development Manager Tim Armes foresees many changes coming. 'The level of the market over the next couple of years is perhaps £30-50 million. In years to come there'll be co-funded programming and then tailor-made programmes. And barter will come: instead of co-funding or sponsoring a programme, a client may produce a programme, e.g. a soap opera, and sell it to a TV company not for money but for advertising airtime. At present it's illegal to act as a broker of airtime – according to the ITC. If it were allowed, the client could use airtime or sell the airtime on. That's even further ahead.'

The Role of Research[17]

Programme sponsorship is still in the early stages of its development, but we need to remind ourselves that there is more of it than the majority of television viewers are aware. This is because it is much more prominent on satellite television.

For example, in July 1991 between 25% and 50% of the combined output of Sky Sport and Screensport was produced in association with sponsors. The Wimbledon Championships attracted different sponsors on each channel. On Sky, coverage was sponsored by three companies, Export 33, Elmlea and Head; while on Screensport regular score bulletins were sponsored by Rolex. Outside sport, the programmes *FT Business Weekly* and *Fashion TV* were sponsored by Max Factor.

As a result of this growing number of sponsorships, an increasingly large role is being taken by research, in relation to the sponsors' principal objectives, 'targeting' and 'synergy'. In advance of a sponsorship, the questions are, 'what is the programme's target audience?' and 'how does that audience perceive the programme being considered for sponsorship?' After the sponsored programme has been broadcast, the questions must include, 'who watched it?', 'did they notice the sponsorship?', 'did they think it was appropriate?', 'were they irritated by any aspect of it?', 'was awareness of the sponsor raised by the sponsorship?' and 'was the image of the sponsor enhanced (or changed in the hoped-for direction) by the sponsorship?'

All of these questions are easier to ask than to answer, but much research is now under way to find ways of answering these questions among others. The point is that research matters. It is important to know, for example, that National Power's sponsorship of the 1990 World Cup caused considerable irritation among viewers, because of its high profile supplementary advertising; and that the consumer advice programme *Wish You Were Here* lost overall credibility as a result of Thomas Cook's involvement. Such research provides lessons that have evidently been learnt by Thames Television and by Sony.

Questions and Prospects

In the whole field of sponsorship, television programme sponsorship is the newest area of growth, so that it has been possible in this brief survey to see the patch entire. But when it comes to predicting the pattern of future growth, the newness of the patch is the problem, for it is still too soon to say. However, some possible developments have been mentioned in the course of our survey of the field, and these will now be considered more closely.

Programme sponsorship, in John Marchant's words, 'has come of age'; the regulations are in place and all those involved, whether broadcasters or sponsors, are benefiting. The questions now to be answered about sponsorship are: how fast will it grow? will the regulations change in such a way as to affect this growth? what developments will the sponsors be pressing for? what developments will producers wish to see happen? what developments will be welcome to the broadcasters? what changes may be expected at the BBC? how will all these interests be reconciled? and how will the viewing public be affected?

How fast will sponsorship grow?

Given expenditure on television sponsorship of £5 million in 1990, £12 million in 1991 and £20 million in 1992, Chilton's prediction of £50 million in the mid-1990s seems quite feasible. There were 37 programmes offered by the ITV network for sponsorship in 1992, and there will be others offered by Channel 4 and the satellite channels. In future years the number is certain to grow.

John Marchant's prediction of annual expenditure rising to £150 million does not seem likely for the foreseeable future, whether it is expressed as 75 Rugby World Cup equivalents each year or in some other coin. However, when the current economic recession is a memory, in the second half of the 1990s, expenditure on television sponsorship might well reach £50 million, which would be just under 3% of 1990's spot advertising expenditure and would, we may assume, be a smaller proportion of advertising expenditure at that future date.

On the other hand, expenditure on sports sponsorship in this country reached £180 million in 1990. And so, if television sponsorship takes an increasing share of the event sponsorship market, John Marchant's prediction *for the long term* may look less futuristic at the start of the 21st Century.

Will the regulations change?

There will be pressure brought to bear on the ITC by potential sponsors for further relaxation in its *Code of Programme Sponsorship,* and no doubt changes will follow. But they are likely to be minor from the audience's viewpoint, such niceties as the way a sponsor's logo is presented – how it moves, how it is associated with the company name or a voice-over, how long it stays on screen, etc. However, such things are important to the advertisers, because a firm distinction is certain to be maintained between sponsorship and advertising, between what is permitted in sponsorship credits and what is permitted in commercial breaks.

What is ultimately possible will be governed by European regulations, but there are already real differences between the countries of Europe in what is allowed. For example, the Italian legislation specifically does not impose any limits on the inclusion of promotional messages or indeed on the actual presence of the sponsoring brand within the television programme.[18]

Nonetheless, this country has a strong tradition of controlling its television by regulation, so that what changes occur are still likely to be small, more in the detail than the overall approach.

What developments will the sponsors be pressing for?

Apart from changes in the regulations, the sponsors will be pressing for opportunities in three areas.

First, in Ian Schoolar's words, 'Companies will be looking for opportunities to link up with independent producers to develop proposals to make programmes, *provided that* there's also a link up with a broadcaster to ensure that the programme gets on air.' In other words, they will be looking for co-production opportunities.

Second, they will want direct access to ITV's future central scheduler (or network scheduler) who may have £600 million at his/her disposal for buying programmes. The chance to offer direct backing for programme-making or to sponsor television coverage of a special event through one central office will create opportunities that some sponsors will not wish to refuse.

Third, they will press for longer term planning and scheduling by the broadcasters, so that sponsorship negotiations fit in more easily with their own long term planning and budgeting.

It does not seem likely, for the foreseeable future, that there will be much pressure for barter deals or the broking of airtime.

What developments will producers wish to see happen?

The number of independent producers will doubtless always be large, but the marketplace of the future is likely to comprise a small number of large firms and a very large number of small, some very small, firms. A large number will always be on the lookout for sponsorship money to finance their programme-making proposals.

Channel 4 will not at present entertain such arrangements, but it does seem predictable that ITV channels will be agreeable to tripartite negotiations with a sponsor and a producer – provided that they retain some form of editorial control. And Channel 4 will have to reconsider its position.

What developments will be welcome to the broadcasters?

The broadcasters seem likely to welcome any developments in respect to sponsorship, *provided that they retain editorial control of their programmes and are convinced that their viewers believe that they do so.*

A variety of co-production deals are certain to evolve in the future, and co-production arrangements with advertisers/sponsors are likely to be among them.

The broadcasters will look for a larger financial return from their coverage of sponsored events. To quote Richard Holliday again, 'Without the television rights, the whole thing is dead. We're going to be saying, "we don't just want the broadcasting rights".'

What changes may be expected at the BBC?

In this area, nothing real. The climate in which the future of the BBC is to be considered is already changing, and it now seems unlikely that any government will cajole the BBC into accepting either advertising or direct sponsorship.

We may therefore expect some tidying up, when the Charter comes up for revision in 1996, so that the BBC's ability to accept money from a sponsor to defray the costs of a free-standing performance organised by the BBC is explicitly declared, rather than a matter of interpretation. Such revision may also leave the way open to further changes in the longer term.

How will all these interests be reconciled?

This question may be put in an alternative way that has already been hinted at: is the ITV companies' insistence on retaining editorial control of their programmes compatible with the growth of sponsorship on the scale that has been envisaged? This is the heart of the matter.

The answer cannot be a matter of fact. It must be a matter of perception and belief. But let us start with two facts. It is a fact that this country has a long and proud tradition of public service broadcasting. As a corollary of this, it is a fact that the British system of broadcasting is more subject to regulation and control than any other with which it may sensibly be compared.

There is a possibility (some would say a real danger) that the winds of the free market, directed by Mrs Thatcher's government at the broadcasting community, may blow away the most deeply held, and externally respected, values of that community. But it is most unlikely. Far more probable is that those values will be subtly and slowly, but inevitably, modified by changes in the outside world.

If this is so, then sponsors may be expected to respect the claims of the broadcasters to retain editorial control of their programmes and not to apply the pressures toward banality and blandness in programme-making that have been evident in the USA. For the situation in the US is very different: there broadcasters have to supply more than 200 channels with programmes and there the advertisers have a much stronger purchase on the broadcasters, who sell them 13 minutes of advertising time in each hour of programming.[19]

How will the viewing public be affected?

On the surface, very little; but under the surface they will benefit.

It seems likely, despite all the prophecies of doom that followed the 1988 Broadcasting Bill and the 1990 Broadcasting Act and that preceded and followed the 1991 ITV franchise auction, that British television viewers will continue to enjoy a range, variety and quality of programmes not very dissimilar to what they have known in the past. Changes there are bound to be, but they are likely to be less violent and less perturbing than the Cassandras have predicted.

This is simply because established (and cherished) social institutions and deeply held (and widely respected) cultural values change far more slowly than most politicians and other ephemeral commentators suppose.

But the economy of broadcasting **is** changing, and new sources of finance **have** to be found to supplement the old. Sponsorship is one of these new sources, which looks likely to provide an increasing share of the funding that future programme-makers will require. Hence, because sponsorship will support programme-making, under the surface (behind the screen) the viewers will unquestionably benefit.

NOTES

1. The paper quoted from is *Clarifying the Details of the New Code Governing Programme Sponsorship* by Frank Willis, Director of Advertising and Sponsorship at the ITC. It was presented to a conference on Sponsorship organised by the Institute for International Research (IIR) Ltd in September 1991.

2. All the interviews referred to in this chapter were carried out in the Autumn of 1991 and only Alan Chilton (see Note 10) was referred to also at a later date. John Marchant was interviewed as Sponsorship Controller at Granada Television.

3. The interview at PowerGen was with Diane Long, Head of Corporate Communications.

4. The interview concerning National Power's sponsorship was with Ian Schoolar, who was their Corporate Communications Director at the relevant time.

5. The interview at Sony was with Paul Campbell, their PR Manager in October 1991.

6. The interview concerning Croft Port' sponsorship was with Paul Freeman, UK Brand Manager for Croft Port.

7. The quotations concerning Lloyds Bank's sponsorship are taken either

from an interview with David Goldesgeyme, Sponsorship Manager, or from a Lloyds Bank News Release dated 6 February 1990.

8. The precise figure for spot advertising expenditure in 1990 is £1,753 million, net of commission. The gross figure, therefore, is just over £2 billion.

9. Richard Holliday was interviewed as Sponsorship Controller at LWT.

10. Alan Chilton is Sponsorship Manager at Scottish Television. He is also Chairman of the ITVA Sponsorship Committee.

11. Tim Brady was interviewed as Head of Sponsorship at Thames Television.

12. The quotations about Channel 4 are taken either from an interview with Stewart Butterfield or from an internal Channel 4 document 'Channel 4: Code of Programme Sponsorship' dated 28 March 1991.

13. The quotations about BBC policy are all from an interview with Patricia Hodgson, Head of the BBC's Policy & Planning Unit.

14. Quotations concerning Media Dimension's work are taken either from an interview with Nicholas Bryant and Paul Green or from publicity material issued by them.

15. Quotations concerning Wood Lynds are taken from an interview with Mark Wood.

16. This section is based on an interview with Tim Armes, Development Manager of The Sponsorship Rating Company.

17. Factual material in this section is taken from *Using Research to Enhance and Evaluate the Effect of Programme Sponsorship*, a paper presented by Susan Tindale, Marketing Development Manager of AGB Sponsorship, to the IIR Conference.

18. The Italian reference is taken from *Maximising the Potential and Avoiding the Dangers of TV Sponsorship – Learning from the European Experience*, a paper presented by Roger Coombes, Marketing Director, Countline, Nestlé (Perugina), to the IIR Conference.

19. However, a contrary view is expressed by Steve Barnett. 'As sponsorship money becomes a larger element of channel revenue and of independent producers' survival, the greater will be the temptation to create programmes consistent with potential sponsors' values: wholesome, decent, family and, above all, uncontroversial.' See Barnett, 'Switching on the sponsors', *The Guardian*, 18 March 1991.